Latin Thunder, My Journey off the Top Rope!

Latin Thunder

Editing: Mindy Brogly

Cover Design: Dony Tristanto
Back Cover Photo: Matt Tucker

For My Dad Jorge. We miss you greatly.

Chapter 1: Seeing "Wildfire"
Chapter 2: Border Town
Chapter 3: River Town
Chapter 4: Pumping Iron
Chapter 5: Rocky Brewer
Chapter 6: Wake Up Call
Chapter 7: Dead End
Chapter 8: Percy's Book
Chapter 9: Picking a Camp
Chapter 10:Skandar Akbar
Chapter 11: Alex Porteau
Chapter 12: JBL
Chapter 13: Crockett
Chapter 14: Leaving Texas
Chapter 15: Back to Iowa
Chapter 16: The Sportatoruim
Chapter 17: Power Plant
Chapter 18: Discovering The Indy's
Chapter 19: Sam Houston
Chapter 20: Lenny Lane
Chapter 21: Hector Guerrero
Chapter 22: Learning the Ropes
Chapter 23: Treach Phillips Jr.
Chapter 24: Harley Race
Chapter 25: Blue Collar
Chapter 26: Back to Camp
Chapter 27: Fly on the Wall
Chapter 28: Opportunity Lost
Chapter 29: Layoff
Chapter 30: Bockwinkel

Chapter 31: Black & Brave
Chapter 32: No Limits
Chapter 33: Turning Heel
Chapter 34: Troy Peterson
Chapter 35: IPW
Chapter 36: Lucha
Chapter 37: Lesson from Seth Rollins
Chapter 38: Real Estate
Chapter 39: Marriage & Family
Chapter 40: Last Chance
Chapter 41: Thanking Skandar
Chapter 42: Too Little, Too Late
Chapter 43: Baby Boy
Chapter 44: Briscoe and Ross
Chapter 45: Hacksaw
Chapter 46: Luchador
Chapter 47: The Character
Chapter 48: My Hero Passes
Chapter 49: Meeting "Wildfire"

CHAPTER ONE

Seeing "Wildfire"

I had arrived in Dallas Texas Wednesday after a long fifteen hour drive. I wanted to get a workout in before my match. Skandar Akbar had given me the date for my bout at the Sportatorium a few weeks back. I went to Mr. Akbars wrestling school at Doug's Gym Wednesday night and got in the ring after a long layoff. I saw Cody there and a few new students. I had a good workout where I tried to reacquaint my back to the hard slams of a wrestling ring.

Now it was Friday night and I was getting ready for my first ever match. And what a place to have your first match! Nashville has its solid country gold names that are still echoed with reverence. Hank Williams, Cash, Jennings, Waylon & Willie. They have their Grand Old Opry.

We have those solid gold names in wrestling also. Like a beautiful black and white photo they stirred us. They resonated with us. In Texas wrestling we also had the Sportatorium.

When you stood in the Sportatorium you knew they had ALL passed through there. Fritz, Wahoo, Flair, Race, Thesz, Brody, Valentine, Rhodes and Murdoch. And the boys. The Von Erich boys.

They had all passed through these doors and laced up their boots in this locker room I was walking into. They had spilled blood and pounded each others bodies in an effort to draw a bigger house than last week.

They laid their shit in because next week they had to be there again. In front of the same fans. They had to make them believe in wrestling and in them.

And now, finally, it was my turn to perform in this arena. After all the setbacks and closed doors my moment was here. I was going to have my first match!

Despite the fact we were living in the "little Mexico" immigrant part of town, my family was one of the first in my school to get cable TV. One Saturday afternoon, at the age of eight, I was alone watching TV in charge of the remote when I came upon Channel 17, the Superstation.

There on TV I heard a very well-spoken man talking about an exciting event that was coming up. It was going to take place inside a ring. The only sport I knew of that took place inside of a ring was boxing. Being Mexican American, I was very familiar with Alexis Arguello, Pepino Cueveas & Roberto Duran, all Latin boxing Hall of Famers. However, this didn't seem to be a boxing event.

Soon enough came two participants and they began fighting furiously. One was a short, balding guy resembling a pit bull whom the announcer called "Mad Dog" Buzz Sawyer. The other guy, the one I liked immediately, was a bright, blond-haired man named "Wildfire" Tommy Rich. I didn't know what I was watching, but I knew I liked it. It had my attention like very few other things in life ever had. *Star Wars*, *Flash Gordon*, Lou Ferrigno in *The Incredible Hulk*, and maybe Christopher Reeves' *Superman* movies had me the same way. Those movies and shows were not real, but this, this was very real!

These guys were larger than life, colorful, and they were engaged in epic battles. They had muscle; they were cool. Since they were on TV, they had to be rich! I found out through my dad that what I was watching was "Lucha", wrestling. Or more specifically Pro Wrestling. It was on every Saturday on Channel 17 from 5:05 p.m. for two solid hours. It came from Atlanta, Georgia, and I was hooked. Tommy "Wildfire" Rich was my favorite wrestler and I cheered him every weekend.

Everyone in my life from that point on knew I was a huge

fan. I never thought at that time all the way through my teens that I was ever going to be a part of this crazy, exciting sport. I mean, after all, who gets to be a pro wrestler? Especially if you're from Muscatine, Iowa, a mid-sized Midwestern town far away from any pro wrestlers. Before the Internet and before anyone ever heard the term independent wrestler, it was a very hard business to break into. But it's amazing what passion, persistence, and the ignorance of youth can make happen. This is my story, one of dreaming, hitting brick wall after brick wall, meeting your heroes, trying to learn a craft, and having fun along the way. I hope you enjoy it.

CHAPTER TWO

Border Town

Mom and Dad

My Dad is from the Mexican side of a border town, Piedras
Negras. My mom is from the Texas side, Eagle Pass. My paternal
grandmother was born in Texas as my great grandfather was
fleeing the Mexican government; he was a revolutionist fighting
against Porfirio Diaz's forces. Sentenced to be shot, he pretended
to be dead among the corpses and somehow got away. After
crossing the Rio Grande when the border wasn't much of a
border, my grandmother Dora was born.

Since she was a legal U.S. citizen when my dad was a teen,
he, his sister, and my Grandma settled into Eagle Pass and my
dad was able to easily get his green card. He began traveling
through California and the Pacific Northwest while working the
whole time and enjoying the wandering life. It must have been a
beautiful country to see in the early 60's. I always enjoyed
hearing my dad tell those stories of working and traveling, seeing

8

the country, young and free. It sounded cool.

Every once in a while when he missed home or ran a little short of money, he'd come back to Eagle Pass where the Ramon family were his neighbors. He'd work at the movie theater and any odd job he could find. Once, he even got a job as an extra on the John Wayne movie, *The Alamo,* which was being filmed nearby. He always told stories of his time on the set, calling John Wayne, "The Duke," like they were old friends. He said the co-star, Richard Widmark, and Wayne would always argue about how Wayne wanted Widmark to play the role.

One day while dad was managing a local movie theater, a job recruiter showed up saying he was looking for workers for a factory in Iowa. He told dad he heard Mexicans were hard workers and he had a job waiting for any able bodied man willing to head up north. Dad always felt he had a bleak future if he stayed in Eagle Pass. Nowadays, it's thriving due to the natural gas boom, but at that time there were little manufacturing jobs. He took the guy's card and headed north with his brother-in-law soon after to Muscatine, Iowa. Sure enough, as soon as they walked into the human resources office, the guy said, "Eagle Pass, Eagle Pass right? I got a job for you, just like I said." The recruiter put him and my uncle up at the local YMCA for housing and my dad began a thirty-five plus year career at the tire retread factory. My dad ended up marrying the girl next door, my mom, Evangelina Ramon. They had a nice wedding in Eagle Pass on New Year's Eve in 1966 and then headed back north to the cold of Iowa to start a new life.

CHAPTER THREE
River Town

Growing up in Muscatine was a great childhood-boring, but great. Growing up Mexican American always made me feel a bit different, but in a good way. I knew two different cultures. My Spanish wasn't great and I didn't work to improve it, but I certainly was proud of my Hispanic roots. My family and I loved our yearly trips to see our family in Eagle Pass, and Texas was always associated with good times.

As I grew up, I did all the things most kids do. I played little league, a year of football, and ran track. I enjoyed them all and was a pretty decent athlete, but I wasn't really a fan of any of the sports I played. The only sport I really followed the way other kids followed basketball or baseball was pro wrestling. I watched it religiously, any hour it was on TV, any promotion. I knew who held what belts, who were the revered legends of the sport, the veterans, and the title holders.

I was a painfully skinny kid, 101 pounds in seventh grade despite being five foot seven or so. I always admired strong, powerful-looking wrestlers. One of my favorites was Tony "Mr. USA " Atlas. A black bodybuilder with an incredible physique, he was on the very first live wrestling card my dad ever took me to. Atlas was a staple on Channel 17's Georgia Championship Wrestling and then later in the WWF. I loved his tag team with Rocky Johnson. I vividly remember them defeating the Wild Samoans for the tag title on the USA network. Soon after I was watching TV with my parents and there was a commercial for a

11

wrestling card advertising Tony Atlas! Amazingly, my parents talked a little about where the card was going to be held at and were actually considering taking me! Sure enough, Dad got us two tickets. He drove to the box office at the Palmer Auditorium in Davenport, Iowa and got me a front row seat and himself a second row ticket right behind me.

I found out it was an AWA card, a group based out of Minneapolis I had read about in the wrestling magazines at my local newsstand, Cohn's. I had never seen an AWA TV show to be honest, but I had read about many of the guys who were wrestling that night. But the person I was most excited about seeing was Tony Atlas. Sure enough, he came out for the third match and was as huge as he seemed on TV. I patted his enormous arms as he walked to the ring and was mesmerized when he military pressed his opponent, Steve Regal, winning the victory with ease. The rest of the card was just as exciting as Jumping Jim Brunzell defeated "Sheik" Adnan Al Kassie. In the main event, the Fabulous Ones defeated Nick Bockwinkel and Mr. Saito in an exciting fast-paced, tag team bout. On the way home, Dad broke one of his driving rules and left the dome light on just so I could read the program.

CHAPTER FOUR

Pumping Iron

Being so skinny always bothered me. When I was in sixth grade my older brother, Ismael, got a set of ten pound dumbbells to help him improve his baseball arm. He let me use them as much as I wanted. The next year my other older brother, Jorge, had a friend, Santos, who gave me a curl bar with two fifteen pound weights. I wore those pieces of equipment out over the next few years.

I still was skinny, but little by little I put on some weight and some muscle. My freshman year though was the big breakthrough. At my dad's company, they gave employees a fifty-percent discount on any Y membership. The local Y was only four blocks away from our home and a teen membership was only forty-four dollars. With Dad's Bandag discount, a yearly membership only cost me twenty-two dollars!

I knew the weight room was as basic as can be, but compared to what I was using at home it was like training at Muscle Beach in Venice, California! The weight room had a universal machine where I could do a few cable exercises and dips, but the free weight room was hardcore. A squat rack, dumbbells, two Olympic benches, a pull up bar, t bar rows, and more Olympic free weights than I could ever need.

All this looked like it was over thirty years old, but I actually thought it was pretty cool all this stuff was so basic. It made me feel I was training like my heroes in Joe Weider's Muscle & Fitness magazine. I loved to read stories of the bodybuilders from the golden age like Arnold Schwarzenegger, Dave Draper, Sergio

14

Oliva, Lou Ferrigno, and others. I especially loved to read about the classic gyms they trained at in California. They sounded like dungeons.

My high school friend Lynn Schenkel and I would go there at least four times a week after school and train. Bench presses, dips, pull ups, bent over barbell rows all while listening to the sounds of 80's hair bands like Def Leppard and Bon Jovi. Those workouts went a long way in helping me build some quality muscle, learn how to train, build some discipline, and learn the joy of working out. Soon I went from that 101 pounds in seventh grade to 165 pounds my sophomore year.

I still had an intense love of wrestling and remember going down to the gym on Saturday mornings by myself. Even during the week it was usually just one or two people other than Lynn and I training, but Saturdays there was never anyone in the weight room. I would turn half the lights off and crank that rock music up. I imagined I was Nikita Kololff during those intense training sessions he held in a dungeon when he was preparing for his series of matches against Ric Flair during the Great American Bash tour. The local Y was becoming my dungeon, my place I found so very comfortable. I enjoyed the solitude, the lack of a team. It was just me or me and Lynn in there training, growing. Every month brought a little progress in how much weight we could put up or how we looked.

Once again, I had found an activity that seemed like a sport to me, but was not very mainstream. I couldn't find my heroes from bodybuilding like Lee Haney or Rich Gaspari being covered on SportsCenter. I had to go to my local newsstand in order to get my fix, my information on this activity and sport I found so much more interesting than traditional sports. Every Friday when Cohn's got their new shipments in, there I was buying my copies of wrestling and muscle magazines. Instead of begging Dad for a baseball glove, I asked him to take me to the local GNC and asked if he could buy me some protein powder. Like he supported my brother Jorge with boxing, my brother Ismael in baseball, and my younger sister Isabel in her church and school activities Dad supported me. He bought me my gym membership and my supplements and shook his head at all those magazines of crazy wrestlers and bodybuilders in his house.

As I got older, I found a part-time job at the fast-food chain Hardees when I turned sixteen. I began to think about what I was going to do when I finished High School. I was enjoying life as a teenager, meeting a whole new group of friends at the restaurant, making some money, and getting my license. I didn't go out for track my junior year, focusing instead on my weightlifting and work. I was doing all the things most kids do at that age, especially in the type of town I grew up in.

I was still going to the Y and had even found a new gym down the road called Park Avenue Fitness run by a local bodybuilder named Doug McChonnaha. Doug had competed in Mr. Iowa, ran a successful business, had a five-hundred pound bench, and had a smoking hot girlfriend all while still being around twenty-five years old. His gym was great, because even though there could be a dozen or so people in there training at one time, those dozen people were all serious about their lifting. The gym was hardcore where chalk, heavy weights, Guns and Roses, and Metallica were welcome.

A lot of the guys had good jobs, were good athletes, and all seemed to have active social lives. They weren't losers. I enjoyed going there and, like all gyms I've ever been to, they made me feel welcome. They could see I enjoyed the iron and took it seriously. I made some new friends and acquaintances that I still have today.

Doug was the very first guy that I ever met who actually knew a few pro wrestlers on a casual level. He had met Ken Patera and Road Warrior Animal through his gym and supplement business. He also had a friend who was a bouncer in Iowa City who wrestled for a minor local pro wrestling group called Ringside Championship Wrestling, Hatchet Jack. Jack had a reputation of being a legit bad ass bouncer you didn't want to mess with in the college bar scene. Doug and lots of the other gym members were also fans of wrestling, not like me, but they enjoyed watching wrestling and knew all the big names.

About the summer before my senior year, it slowly began to

grow in my mind that maybe I could be a pro wrestler. I was a huge fan-bigger than any of my friends. Only Chad Ash from high school was as big of a fan as I was. Also, I really enjoyed hitting the weights and that seemed to help you stand out in the world of wrestling. I was a decent athlete. Wrestling involved a lot of travel and unlike many   people I enjoyed the thought of seeing the world and getting paid for it. The idea of being on TV, being someone special seemed cool. Who else from Muscatine was ever on TV? Why the hell couldn't I try to be a wrestler? Maybe if I committed myself to learning how to get into this business and continued to train hard I could find a way in. That summer began the dream of becoming a pro wrestler-a real pro wrestler. But where to begin? Who in this town of 25,000 people could help me get my foot in the door?

Also, I was only 5 foot 9 and weighed about 180 pounds. I didn't think I was going to get any taller looking at my mom and dad and my two older brothers. My mom was fairly tall for a Hispanic woman, about 5 foot 6. My grandfather on my mom's side was very tall also, about six foot. One of my uncles, Tio Polo, got my grandfather's height, but it didn't look like me or my brothers were ever going to be six foot tall. All the wrestlers I read about in Pro Wrestling Illustrated were a minimum of two hundred pounds. Light Heavyweights like Tim Horner or Brad Armstrong were supposed to be "smaller," but they all weighed at least two hundred pounds and had plenty of muscle.   Only in the giant-sized world of pro wrestling would a man who weighed around two hundred pounds be considered light. So, my goal was to hit that mark-two hundred pounds. I wasn't going to get any taller, but it seemed like there were a decent amount of wrestlers who were around the five foot nine inch mark. So, I didn't think that would be a deal breaker.

As I finished up my senior year, I got a girlfriend named Sarah. We met at Hardees and dated for the next several years. She and all my friends thought my crazy dream of being a pro wrestler was alright, maybe even kind of neat. However, they were as stumped as I was on how to break into it.

I continued working at Hardees and making my two hundred

17

dollar payment on my 1987 Chevy Camaro that I just had to have in the fall of 1990. Dad suggested I buy something cheaper, because it cost $6,500. He knew the anchor a monthly payment that size would have on my life and options. But like most young kids, I didn't think of that.

I worked a ton of hours while finishing up my senior year, working every weekend and at least three times a week. I was bringing home around $140 a week at the time, maybe a little more and easily made my car payment. But I wasn't saving anything, and I wasn't making any extra payments. I didn't really see the need as I wasn't having any luck finding a wrestling school or anywhere tangible I could call or write to.

I almost didn't graduate from high school, because I was late to my first hour math class so many times, a class that I needed to pass in order to get my diploma. I was working until 11:30 p.m. most school nights and I was having trouble waking up early enough to get to class on time. The assistant principal sat me down and let me know if I was late one more time I would be dropped form the class and unable to graduate. He told me if I had any plans for the future not having a diploma would severely limit them. I knew he was right, neither of my parents had graduated from high school. They both dropped out to work and help out their family. Dad had dropped out in sixth grade. His father had passed away at a young age when Dad was only two years old. He spent his teen years working to help his struggling single mother, my grandmother Dora. He worked at the Coca-Cola bottling plant in Piedras Negras and any other work to help the household.

All my parents had ever asked from us was to finish high school. I knew it wasn't too much to ask and it would break my parents' hearts if I didn't finish. The assistant principle Mr. Morgan asked me what I had planned for after high school. I had an Ultimate Warrior t-shirt on and told him my plans and dreams of being a pro wrestler. To his credit, Mr. Morgan didn't laugh at me or discourage me. He simply told me a diploma would be a needed backup plan, and it would be silly to screw things up just because I couldn't wake up on time.

I didn't change my hours, but I did buckle down and made it a priority to get to school on time. I ultimately graduated in 1991. I was done with school, I had my backup plan. I didn't disappoint my parents and I was looking forward to the next stage in life.

CHAPTER FIVE

Rocky Brewer

Sometime in 1991, I began regularly watching the local wrestling promotion Ringside Championship. It was different watching this program, now I was studying it. Before, I used to watch the program as a pure fan and, while I watched it and enjoyed it, I didn't think much of it if I missed an episode. Their TV production values were not great compared to WCW that was now on the TBS Superstation time slot owned by Ted Turner or Vince McMahon's WWF. But as I studied it closer, I had to give them their due. They had TV on a real channel, the local Fox affiliate. They were on a good time slot, Saturday mornings I think, and a replay late at night around midnight or so. They did interviews and had legitimately trained wrestlers with their top star being Rocky Brewer.

I had seen a couple of the local shows they ran in Muscatine as fundraisers for the hometown semi pro baseball team at Central Middle School. They progressively were drawing less fans over the years. A lot of their wrestlers seemed to be out of shape and older; some of them just didn't look like stars. I couldn't put my finger on why I felt that way, but that was my perception as a fan. But again, they had some things going for them. Rocky Brewer was a decent-sized guy who seemed to be a good wrestler; he wasn't Ric Flair, but he was good. Also, I really took note when I saw they had a young wrestler working for them named The Nightstalker. He looked to be around six foot five or more, had a great build, and was a good athlete. He also had Ox Baker as his manager. Ox was a guy who had a memorable role in the Kurt Russell cult hit *Escape from New York*. Ox was at the end of his career and pretty beaten-up, but I knew Ox Baker was a part of wrestling. He had been in the magazines as long as I could remember. I'd seen him on TV in Georgia Championship wrestling in the early 80's. He seemed to be a main eventer; he had an incredible look in his prime with his long Fu Manchu mustache and great size. He looked like a real-life video game character you had to fight against. What he was doing in this promotion was beyond me, but he was there.

When the Nightstalker showed up on national TV in WCW with Ox Baker as his manager, I knew this local promotion might be my ticket into the wrestling business! Maybe it was a great place to start, get trained, and get some experience in the minor leagues before trying one of the larger more well-known territories that were still around during that time such as Texas or Memphis. As I continued watching the show, I noticed they had an address to send fan mail to that was in Charlotte, Iowa. Charlotte is a tiny town outside of Clinton, Iowa. Eventually, they also started saying they had a wrestling school you could get information about at that address!

So, I sat down and wrote a letter to that address inquiring about the school. I got a response back stating they trained in Clinton, Iowa, and gave me a phone number to call. I called the number and who answered but Rocky Brewer, the journeyman wrestler I had seen headline all the cards at Central Middle School! Rocky told me over the phone that yes they had a school and I was welcome to come up and train. He had class on Saturdays in the morning. The school would cost $3,000 and, if I completed the school, I was guaranteed my first match with Ringside Championship Wrestling. I told Rocky I didn't have $3,000, but I could make payments. He said that was fine, and we agreed upon $300 monthly payments and I would have my first payment the day I started.

I really didn't know what to expect that first day at camp, but, to be honest, I didn't take it as seriously as I should have. I really wanted to be a wrestler, and I was going to the gym regularly. However, I wasn't exactly tearing it up in there. I still weighed around 185 pounds, was 18 years old, and had very little knowledge or understating of the wrestling business. I really didn't have any idea what I was getting into. I expected it to be a little tough, but not that bad. I had no idea what kind of rude awakening Rocky Brewer had in store for me when welcoming me into the sacred fraternity of professional wrestling.

CHAPTER SIX

Wake Up Call

Thanks to the beauty of You Tube, the Internet, and social media I now know a lot more about Rocky Brewer than I did in the early 90's. At the time, I still really didn't know just how legit Rocky was as I had never seen him on national TV. If I had seen him even being used as enhancement talent or a preliminary wrestler, I would have had a better understanding of where he stood in the wrestling business.

It turned out that Rocky was from the Clinton, Iowa, area originally and did break into the sport in the 1970's. I don't think I can describe to non wrestling fans just how difficult that was to do in that era. It may have been the most difficult era to break into in the history of the business. There are stories after stories of guys being stretched, put in painful submission holds, exercised to exhaustion, and just plain beaten up trying to break into wrestling during the 70's. If you didn't have a family member or connection into the industry, you paid a tremendous price. The industry was so secretive and protective of its inner workings that it didn't let anyone in who it felt would possibly expose the business.

Thanks to a great Facebook page called World Class Memories, I have seen Rocky's name listed in the card results form the Sportatorium in Dallas, Texas. He wrestled first or second match often against big names such as Jimmy "Superfly" Snuka. I also saw on You Tube in the early 80's some matches from the Southwest territory in San Antonio where Rocky is wrestling against Gino Hernandez. In addition, I've seen newspaper clips of him working the Florida territory run by the legendary wrestler/promoter Eddie Graham. He also worked Nick Gulas's territory in Tennessee and feuded with a young Bobby Eaton. So, I can say without a shadow of a doubt now that Rocky was legit. He has a tremendous amount of respect from me for breaking into the business and being a full-time pro in his prime.

But in 1991 I didn't know any of that as I drove to Clinton, Iowa, from Muscatine for my first workout. Rocky met me at the address we talked about. He was about five foot eleven or so and weighed around 240-250 pounds with a little extra around the middle, but he had a solid, strong build. He looked to be around forty years old. He was cordial to me, shook my hand, and took my $300. We went inside the building that was basically a small warehouse space with a dirty, old ring that was not very well lit. It was kind of chilly being the fall in Iowa. Rocky told me we were going to do some warm ups and had me grab a broom and sweep up the ring. I swept up the dusty, dirty ring and Rocky proceeded to show me where there were a few old buckets if I needed them later in case I threw up.

That was the very first indicator that I was probably unprepared for what was about to happen. I had never thrown up doing any kind of exercising, so I kind of brushed off his comments in my mind. Rocky said that we were going to start by doing some somersaults as a warm up. I thought this would be a piece of cake.

Rocky had me begin the somersaults going in one direction of the ring. I was breezing through them when at around the five minute mark my lower back was starting to hurt. I figured this warm up should be finishing up soon, but instead Rocky had me turn around and start doing the somersaults the other way. Now, my wind was starting to get labored and my lower back increasingly began to hurt more and more. As I was beginning to think about quiting, Rocky began to say something over and over again. It was a phrase I had never heard on TV or read in any wrestling magazine, "So you wanna be a rassler?" He wasn't being condescending. He wasn't being a jerk, and he wasn't getting in my face. But he kept clapping his hands together and saying it as I pushed my body to continue, "So you wanna be a rassler?"

After about 15 minutes of continuous somersaults, I felt the need to grab one of those buckets that Rocky pointed to early. I reached for one and began to throw up in this old, dirty bucket that had been sitting in this warehouse for who knows how long. As I finished throwing up, Rocky told me to keep going and I did. I wasn't in the best shape, but I was young. I just couldn't imagine going home and telling everyone that I quit that soon, before I even learned something.

So, I kept going, somersault after somersault. I threw up at least two more times, the last time being just dry heaves. My lower back was killing me, but I kept going.   After probably a full forty-five minutes of the somersaults with Rocky asking me, "So you wanna be a rassler?", Rocky told me to take a break. Next, he had me do some up downs, some push ups, and a few other exercises. After that he finally showed me a wrestling move that looked familiar to me, a lock up. We locked up and he had me push him from one side of the ring to another over and over again. My shoulders were hurting, but I was just thankful I wasn't doing somersaults. This at least resembled something I saw in a wrestling match.

After a total of an hour and a half, Rocky said that was it for today. We talked a little after the workout and I asked him some questions. I asked him about some things I had seen on TV the week before when he got into a brawl with another wrestler. I wanted to know how they did that. Rocky politely brushed me off and said he just lost his temper and he needed to stop doing that as the promoter wasn't happy about them fighting in the studios. To every question I asked Rocky seemed to imply that everything was real, he wasn't smartening me up to anything. I was confused on the way to my car. I got the impression from Rocky I was asking too many questions. At my job at Hardees, my bosses loved it when I asked a lot of questions. At the gym, the older guys thought it was a sign you wanted to learn if you asked a lot of questions. I certainly didn't get the impression from Rocky he liked me talking so much. We agreed to meet the following Saturday morning and he said a couple guys might join us who were also students.

CHAPTER SEVEN

Dead End

After the initial wake-up call with Rocky during the drive home and all that following week, I did a lot of thinking. What was interesting was I never thought about not showing up the next week. I just realized this was a serious business, and the people involved were not going to let anyone in who didn't take it as seriously as they did. I gave up all the silly and ridiculous thoughts I had that wrestling school was going to be like going to acting school or learning how to "fake" things. I also realized I was going to have to be in great shape for this. Rocky didn't injure me. I didn't have to go to the doctor. I just was being asked to take this seriously and be prepared to work hard.

I was still confused on why he didn't acknowledge that the business was a "work," or predetermined, but I was slowly learning I didn't know as much about this business as I thought I did. Like all young aspiring wrestlers, I was hungry for information, but this industry didn't make it easy at all to find out information.

The following week I met Rocky for training and sure enough two other guys showed up, brothers who drove all the way from Missouri to train. They said they had a five-hour drive to get to camp. I wasn't totally surprised as I realized how hard it was to get anyone to agree to train you, so a person had to be willing to drive wherever their connection to the sport was.

Rocky put us through the exact same workout he did the week before, but amazingly my body handled it much better. Though my lower back was still in pain and I was winded, I didn't throw up. The two guys who showed up had been to camp several times and knew what to expect, but they had trouble getting through the workout since they hadn't been to camp in a while. They never threw up, but they did stop when they just couldn't handle it anymore. They took very brief breaks before continuing. Rocky never yelled at them. He just encouraged them and told them to get moving, and they did. After the conditioning part of training, we moved on to locking up and then learned a bit about how to grab an arm for a wrist lock.

On the way home, I was really proud, happy, and kind of surprised my body handled the conditioning as well as it did.

Truth was unlike a lot of guys my age I had never been pushed, really pushed, in athletics. Amateur wrestlers, high school football players going through two a days in the hot summer, guys who served our military and went through basic training, all would have been better prepared for the camp. They also would have understood the incredible things your body can do if you can push your mind to that place.

The following week we had another training session that went the same as before. I hadn't paid Rocky any more money at that point, but I was saving for another $300 payment. After camp, Rocky told us he wasn't going to have camp the following week as he had to go to Puerto Rico to defend the belt. I knew from the wrestling magazines that Puerto Rico was a hotbed of pro wrestling and one of the remaining places someone who wasn't signed to either WWF or WCW could go. I didn't doubt Rocky, and thought it was pretty cool he was going there. I also had heard him, in between "so you wanna be a rassler" sayings, sing a little Spanish! He would sing this old Spanish song while he was walking around. I can't even remember the name of it, but this told me that this white guy born and raised in Iowa who probably never went to college could speak some Espanol. Where the hell would he have learned it if not from traveling to the island of Puerto Rico? Also, I kind of knew from the magazines that Puerto Rico liked their wrestling violent. It seemed like the pretty boy wrestlers you knew weren't really tough guys never worked Puerto Rico. The only guys who went there seemed to have a legit toughness to them. They were ass kickers, brawlers. They were guys like Bruiser Brody, "Hangman" Bobby Jaggers, and Dick Murdoch. Also, growing up in my Mexican neighborhood we had a neighbor in the late 70's who was Puerto Rican. He was a huge wrestling fan with pictures of Andre The Giant hanging on the wall. His wife said that when they would go to the matches he always had to be restrained by security; he hated the bad guys. If just a few of the fans on the island were like him, it had to be a rough place to wrestle in. That just added to Rocky's mystique to me, if he wrestled there he had to be tough.

I waited a few weeks for Rocky to call me after his tour, but that call never came. I found his number after a while as I had lost his calling information. For you young kids, that's a number we called for a few bucks where you would tell the operator their name and town you were searching in and they would give you their phone number. In Charlotte, Iowa, they didn't have a Rocky Brewer the operator told me, but they did have a Randy Brewer. So, I asked her for that name. Sure enough that was Rocky's real name. I guess after Sylvester Stallone made the famous movie Rocky figured that name was a hell of a lot more marketable than Randy. I would agree.

For the next several months I tried calling Rocky while leaving messages, but he never called back. Knowing the carny image wrestling had, I knew enough to let him know in every message I had another $300 I could pay him. The truth was I was happy to pay anyone who was legitimately able and willing to train me a fair amount, and $3000 sounded reasonable to me. It was a lot, but it was reasonable. It didn't matter, since Rocky never called me back. I think he may have been going through a divorce at that time. I heard rumors later of him living in Puerto Rico doing well for himself as a business owner. I saw a video my friend Mike Ray, a fellow independent wrestler from Muscatine, posted about three to four years back from a show in Davenport where Rocky was given an award for his contributions to wrestling in Southeast Iowa. An award he certainly deserved. Rocky looked good with a shaved head, dressed in a dress shirt and tie, and in great shape.

When I think about Rocky, I always am thankful for the help he gave me. I have nothing but respect and appreciation for him. In a short period of time, he gave me some very valuable lessons about wrestling. I knew as I continued to try to find a school to train me that I had to treat it seriously and with respect. I vowed that, if I got an opportunity to find a good camp, I was going to show up prepared and ready to work and learn. I had been humbled and that was good as the humbling was just beginning.

CHAPTER EIGHT

Percy's Book

After a few months of getting nowhere finding a wrestling school, I got an opportunity in 1992 to go to Nebraska for Hardees by my District Manger George Snakenberg. George was sympathetic to my crazy dream and liked my work at Hardees. He was in his early 30's and looked a little like Nicolas Cage. Fit and intense, George was a runner up in 1980 at the state wrestling meet, winning it his senior year in 1981. Being a state champion in Iowa at amateur wrestling is no easy feat. Iowa has a long tradition of excellence in wrestling producing such legends as Olympic gold medalist Dan Gable.

Since I wasn't getting anywhere finding a wrestling school, I took the opportunity to move to Nebraska to open two new restaurants our franchiser owner Dave Ebbing was constructing. I would be going as an Assistant Manager and making $325 a week in salary. It wasn't bad money and I was flattered George thought so highly of me that he wanted me to be on the team in Nebraska despite my young age. He said if I played my cards right I could possibly be offered a managers job and my own store. That was a career with a salary of $30,000 or so with bonus. It wasn't a glamorous field, but as George said, "My money is as green as anyone else's."

The stores had several setbacks getting opened, but finally in the summer of 1993 I moved to Grand Island, Nebraska. We worked long hours averaging fifteen to sixteen hour days six days a week the first month I was there. The store opened well, but the sales were not what Mr. Ebbing was hoping for. Still, we continued working on the operations and looked to open the second store in nearby Hastings in the winter as planned.

All the while in my limited free time, I still followed wrestling when I could. I finally caught a break when I spotted an ad in Pro Wrestling Illustrated for two mail order books on how to get into wrestling. I sent a check for $15 or $20 to purchase each mail order book. I was suspicious of the ads, but I was desperate and getting nowhere on my own.

Shortly thereafter, I got the first book. It was a complete ripoff. The book was about ten pages long, didn't say who the author was, or list any credentials. It had information such as, "in wrestling there is a lot of travel." Another gem was "working out is very important." No information was given on any address or phone number to contact for training. I felt scammed and could only hope the next book had some worthwhile information.

A few days later came the answer to my questions, just enough information that a young, aspiring wrestler could use if he was serious. It was written by Percy Pringle and Dennis Brent. Percy had made a name for himself in the Dallas territory as a manager before he was signed to the WWF and became the manager of The Undertaker. Yup, Paul Bearer had helped write this book! Instantly, I knew it was legitimate.

Dennis Brent was a name I had heard WCW announcer Jim Ross say countless times. Brent was the editor of the Wrestling Wrap Up, the company's program they sold at house shows. Later, he was in charge of the company's official wrestling magazine sold at newsstands all over the country. Again that was a big sign this mail order book was legit!

The book was full of valuable information in a secretive business, and I soaked it up. It had helpful hints like how to act in the locker room, basically telling you to keep your mouth shut and your ears open. Don't ask a lot of questions when you're first starting out. That made my interactions with Rocky Brewer and his reactions make a lot more sense.

It explained concepts like the fact that if you become a tag team wrestler you may get booked a little less. There is usually only one tag match on each card, for basic, economic reasons. The promoter was going to have to pay four guys, but still only get one match. The book said if you wrestled first or second match you wouldn't do anything outside the ring, no chairs and very little brawling.

I can't describe how important this book was to me, and how generous it was for the two authors to write and offer it to aspiring wrestlers. Sure they were writing it to make a little money, but they didn't have to. The authors had written the book originally in 1989 I believe, toward the end of the World Class era in Dallas. I'm sure they were hurting for money as the territory wasn't on fire anymore. After they wrote the book, their fortunes changed with Percy becoming Paul Bearer and having a long, great career in the WWE. I wrote an e-mail to Paul Bearer, aka Bill Moody, years before he passed away in 2012 to thank him for his help. I shared some of my memories and he responded with some kind words. It felt good to thank him. Brent went on to be editor of both the WCW and later WWE magazine. He co-authored "Stone Cold" Steve Austin's book, since they were friends from the Dallas days. I'm friends with Dennis on Facebook and have thanked him for his help several times.

At the end of the book, it gave a list of wrestling schools you could write to. I studied the list as it included schools from different parts of the country. I think it had a school in Tennessee as well as California and a few other states. The two I zoned in on were the Texas school and the school in Minnesota. I figured the school based in Minneapolis wasn't too far away and I was still staying in the Midwest. The Texas school was in Dallas. I had roots in Texas and was comfortable when we traveled there every summer to visit family. Dallas was a seven-hour drive from my grandma's house in Eagle Pass, but I could try it out and I had a place to stay. I hoped the school would have a connection to Global Wrestling. Global was a prominent promotion that got featured in the magazines, was on ESPN for a long time, and had a lot of young talent get signed by the big two such as the tag team of Harlem Heat.

I wrote to both, sent a picture of myself along with my athletic background, and got a return to sender response from the Minnesota school. I think it was Eddie Sharkey's school, but I'm not one-hundred percent sure. Next came a handwritten letter from Doug's Gym with a return address of Garland, Texas. The letter offered to train me for $1,000! It said they trained once a week on Wednesday. They would guarantee my first match if I completed training. They listed past students such as Dustin Rhodes! That was a big clincher for me. All throughout the 70's, 80's, and 90's if you were to say what wrestler was the most inside, most well-connected wrestler of all, you'd be hard pressed to name anyone better than Dusty Rhodes "The American Dream." I figured if Dusty Rhodes sent his son to Doug's Gym to get trained it had to be legit. The only part that threw me for a loop was it was signed Doug. "Doug who?" I wondered. Oh well, I found my school and I was going to pursue this.

I talked to my friend and boss George at Hardees and told him I was going to have to give my notice. He told me the Grand Island store was mine if I wanted it; I could be the store manager. It wasn't that tough of a decision, but the money did tempt me. I ultimately knew I had no choice-I had to pursue this. George said he understood and wasn't really too surprised I think. We agreed I would stay long enough to help open the Hastings restaurant and leave around February of 1994. I kept my word and drove back home to Muscatine in February. I was going to take a month break; I was burned out from all the hours at Hardees. I would find a job, pay off my Camaro, save my money, hit the gym like never before, and head down to Dallas as soon as I had my money for camp.

CHAPTER NINE

Picking a Camp

I moved back in with my parents. I promptly hit the weights at Doug McConnaha's gym, my old stomping grounds. After I got my tax return money and was ready to find work, my brother Ismael helped get me a job at his employer, CDS, an envelop mail stuffing warehouse in Wilton, Iowa, fifteen minutes away.

I trained with my girlfriend's brother Chris and sometimes his old football buddy Mike would join us. Mike was playing football for Wartburg college and took his lifting seriously. Between the mood at the gym and my training partners, it was a great combination to put on size. I was determined to pack on some muscle, get in good cardio shape, and break that stubborn 200 pound mark.

I was close as I weighed a soft 190. After three months of lifting, eating well, and just the natural growing you're still going through at twenty-one, I hit the 200 pound mark. My bench was good, I was doing 225 for about twelve to thirteen reps, squatting for the first time, 315 pounds for reps. Momentum was building.

The job front was going okay also. I averaged $360 every two weeks take home or so if I worked forty hours a week. But I almost never did that, because I worked overtime every chance I had. Most of the time I averaged $440-$500 bi weekly. Since I was living at home, I made a car payment every other week and was set to pay it off early in June.

I thought it would be a good idea to visit the school in Dallas to see if the camp was in fact a good fit and to get an idea what was in store for me. I called information and got the phone number for Doug's Gym in Dallas off Commerce Street. I called one Wednesday morning after my graveyard shift at work. I asked to talk to Doug and he said they did offer wrestling training and to call back at 7 p.m. He said he would let me talk to Akbar, he was who ran the school. Akbar?!?! He must have meant Skandar Akbar, that bad guy manager I used to see on ESPN on World Class Wrestling battling my heroes the Von Erich boys! That would make sense, Skandar Akbar running a school in Dallas. He was the bad guy manager in Global Wrestling also.

That pumped me up, so I called at 7 p.m. and sure enough I

could recognize that voice-it was Skandar Akbar! I was such a mark I asked him if it was "The General" Skandar Akbar and he said yes. He told me the same things he shared in the letter and said I was welcome to come check out the school any Wednesday night at 7 p.m.

My family was going to be in Texas in the summer, so I headed down there for a week to Eagle Pass. On the way home, I'd check out the school. My trip to Eagle Pass went well visiting family and the day before I headed up to Dallas my uncle Polo and my Dad were looking at maps trying to find Commerce Street. My dad always drove through Fort Worth telling me the traffic in Dallas was terrible, so I was getting nervous. I had never driven through big city traffic like Dallas. Finally, my uncle found Commerce Street. He said the good news was that it was right off I-35, and the bad news was it was right smack in the middle of downtown. I wasn't going to be able to avoid the traffic.

As I drove North on I-35 and past Austin then Waco, I was getting worried. I was driving alone. I was twenty-one and knew I had to do this on my own. When I hit the outskirts of Dallas, this Iowa boy saw those skyscrapers and knew I had to go right in the middle of them. I couldn't let this get in my way, so I just kept going. I managed to navigate the traffic despite my nerves, found my Commerce exit, and proceeded Downtown. I found an expensive-looking hotel, but I didn't have much choice. I wanted to park my car, rest, and walk to Doug's Gym at 7 p.m.

I took a nap, then walked over to the gym. Doug's is kind of a landmark in Dallas. It's a very old school gym, it had no air conditioning, mostly free weights and was no nonsense. Across from the gym is the police station where Jack Ruby killed Lee Harvey Oswald after the Kennedy assassination. Rumor had it Sylvester Stallone said he would have filmed his Rocky movies in it if he had known about it at the time. In the office door was a picture of the late Bruiser Brody, an international wrestling legend. I walked up those old wooden steps and the owner Doug immediately came up to me and said, "Young man, you look like you've been doing some working out. Can I help you?" I told

38

him I was here to talk about wrestling training. Doug walked me through a brick wall that had been busted open with no door to the wrestling ring. There I met Skandar Akbar.

CHAPTER TEN

Skandar Akbar

Skandar grew up in Vernon, Texas, near Wichita Falls. He was a standout high school football player and a strongman who never gave up his love of the iron. You could count on him being reached by phone doing his regular workouts in his home gym every morning. His cousin Doug Eidd owned the gym his wrestling academy was located at. Mid-South promoter and WWE Hall of Fame wrestler "Cowboy" Bill Watts talked about Akbar's unconventional near 400 pound bench press in his book. Akbar would do a clean and jerk of the weight, sit down on the bench then lay down before he even started the conventional part of his bench press.

The legendary shooter and world heavyweight champion Lou Thesz helped train Akbar. Skandar had trouble getting booked initially, so he did what many young wrestlers did, he went to Tennessee. That territory was more forgiving of young, inexperienced wrestlers and he got a lot of work there. He told me years later though that it was often the blind leading the blind. It was a treat if you got to be in the ring with a veteran such as Jacki Fargo, because more often than not you were in there with another newbie.

From there he went back to Texas where Fritz Von Erich helped give him the name Skandar Akbar. He fell in love with his two favorite territories, Mid-South and the Dallas promotion run by Fritz early on, and they fell in love with him. He was reliable and a heat magnet because of his Middle Eastern ethnicity and understanding of wrestling psychology. He was also great with young talent, generous with his advice, and offered a driving companion for those who didn't want to partake in all the drinking and partying on the way to the show or back from it.

Mid-South was a large territory with lots of driving. It entailed Louisiana, Oklahoma, Mississippi, Arkansas, and Houston at times. Watts was known as a great no nonsense promoter; he was all business and paid very well. Fritz's Dallas territory was one of the least demanding in regards to driving; pay wise I've heard conflicting stories, but Mr. Akbar seemed happy. He had a deep respect for both Watts and Fritz and always spoke highly of them.

In Mid-South, he had a great tag team with the amateur standout Danny Hodge, the only amateur wrestler to ever be on the cover of Sports Illustrated. It was one of the few and last times he was cheered. After turning on Hodge, he cemented his bad guy status and reveled in it. He loved getting his heat. He booked Mid-South during periods of time as well and was always respected for his ideas and creativity in helping with angles.

He went on to tag team with Ox Baker in Georgia, worked in Australia for a period of time and was their champion. He was set to get a main event run with Bruno Sammartino in New York for Vince McMahon Sr. when a fellow Texan named Stan Hansen broke Bruno's neck in a match. Skandar settled for a run with Ivan Putski in the smaller markets and said he made plenty of money doing that.

After that he mainly stayed in the Mid-South and Dallas promotions throughout the 1980's. This is where I knew him best from the magazines and a few videos I got my hands on growing up. He was the manager of Devastation Incorporated. His bad guy monsters, or Dragons as he called them, were some of the greatest stars of all time such as Kamala "The Ugandan Giant," One Man Gang, Cactus Jack, and The Missing Link. Some of the biggest stars of all time such as The Undertaker started with him as the masked Punisher.

He was thoroughly in love with the business and often put it before anything else. He just couldn't help it I think. He loved the road and the camaraderie of the sport. I remember shaking my head when he said in a shoot interview he had been away from home working in Georgia, New York, and Australia for several years with just brief breaks to come home and finally gave his notice to come back, because, "I had a very understanding wife, but I didn't want to push it."

After Mid-South was sold to Jim Crockett, Mr. Akbar stayed in Dallas. When World Class went out of business, he worked for Jerry Jarret's USWA. Then he became involved in Global. Mr. Akbar was about sixty years old when I met him for the first time. I was surprised by his brawn and his very light handshake. Mr. Akbar let me sit in on class that day and introduced me to the current Global Light Heavyweight champion Alex Porteau.

Alex had a body type and style similar to Tim Horner or a slightly less muscular Brad Armstrong. He was my height at 5 foot 9 or so and looked to be about 225 pounds very solid with big arms and chest. Alex was from Louisiana and his brown hair was short. He looked like a wrestler-tough.

In the ring that was missing a bottom rope, Alex was training two students, one guy looked to be 6 foot 4 or so and athletic, a big guy. The other student wasn't as good of an athlete, he was six foot and didn't seem to spend time in the gym. The stuff they were doing in the ring looked like pro wrestling, not like the classes I had with Rocky Brewer. They were doing tackles, hitting the ropes, hip tosses, and body slams. Everything Alex did looked great; he was obviously a pro.

I sat on an old couch with Mr. Akbar and watched the action for a while. I asked if the students did any conditioning and Akbar said no, you were expected to do your conditioning on your own. That sounded great to me. I didn't mind doing conditioning, but it was a relief to know I wasn't going to be puking in camp. After a half hour of watching the training, Skandar invited me into his little office where we talked for a few minutes. He reiterated the price was $1,000, a bargain. I could make payments and I could start anytime I wanted. I told him as soon as I paid off my car and saved a few hundred dollars I would start, probably late summer. I asked him if I could could send him $400 in the mail as a start and make $100 payments after that, he said that was fine.

So, I had a plan. I would live with my Grandma in Eagle Pass, which was seven hours away. Since camp was only once a week, I figured I could handle the drive for a while. I shook hands with Mr. Akbar as he walked out with me; we had a deal. He asked his cousin Doug if he had met me and Doug said yes. Mr. Akbar grabbed my shoulders and said, "Take a look at him Doug, he looks great doesn't he. Look at them arms!" Doug agreed, I was feeling good all my hard work in the gym was being noticed by these two veterans of the iron. They both had seen a lot of physiques in their day and their encouraging words meant a lot. I went back to the hotel room where I saw in the news O.J. Simpson's wife had been murdered. I went to bed and drove home the next day.

When I got back home, I went into the bank and made my car payment. I asked the teller if she could tell me the payoff amount, since my next $200 scheduled payment was my last and often the final payment is a slightly different figure. She pulled up the information and told me my payoff was over $1,000! She called up the loan officer and she sent me over to his desk. He proceeded to show me the original loan and said the payment booklet was unfortunately wrong. I really did owe another six months of car payments!

I felt like I had been punched in the gut. I was so close to starting camp and now this! I really don't know what came over me, but I only spent about one minute feeling sorry for myself before I had a quick understanding that this was a small bump in the road. I would delay training for a few months. I would go to Texas with a little less money saved than I had planned, but I was going. This minor detail wasn't going to get in my way. I look back at that moment with a bit of disbelief. It was a mature and patient way to look at a roadblock. It wasn't the way I normally dealt with setbacks at that time in my life. I hadn't read any self-help book that explained how to think about a problem; it was just me deciding.

At the beginning of October, I told my longtime girlfriend Sarah goodbye. We would maintain a long-distance relationship. I got into my Camaro with my brother Ismael who decided to move to Eagle Pass for a fresh start and drove south on I-35 to Dallas. On October 5th, 1994, I started wrestling school.

CHAPTER ELEVEN

Alex Porteau

My first day of camp was pretty basic. I learned how to do a flat back bump. You just kick your legs up and fall back as flat as you can while tucking in your chin. I did that several times and Alex Porteau then had me hit the ropes over and over. It was a bit awkward. I thought I would do it more naturally than I did, but Alex and Skandar said it looked good.

I got taught how to lock up. Mr. Akbar stressed over and over, "Lock up tight, then loosen up." I didn't exactly understand why he was telling me that, but I followed his direction.

That was it for my first day. No puking, lots of encouraging words, not laid back, but just a get your feet wet type of attitude from Alex and Akbar. I did remember Alex asking whether another, newer student was coming back. Mr. Akbar chuckled and said he didn't think so, "I don't think he likes your chops, Alex."

I drove back to the hotel room and could see the top of Texas Stadium. It was pretty cool. After all, it was where the Cowboys played, but more importantly where Kerry Von Erich beat Ric Flair for the NWA World Heavyweight Title in front of 43,000 fans. Texas had a rich history of wrestling, and I had a good feeling about the camp I picked to get my training.

Every week after that I drove seven hours one way to Dallas. I would get a room at the Super 8 in Temple, Texas, roughly a halfway point. I would unpack a few things, take a brief break from driving, then show up at camp around 6 p.m. The training got progressively harder every week, more physical. Alex never took liberties with us, but the slams, suplexes, and hip tosses all got to be more common than the lock ups and running of the ropes.

I clearly remember the workout where Alex was asking me if I wanted to be part of this business. It was about three to four weeks in. As we were getting changed, Alex was telling the senior student in camp Shane, the big six foot five 265 pound guy, that we needed to have a good workout today, a tough one. I wasn't sure what this meant, but I was going to find out.

The workout started as usual with us sparring with Alex. He would call a move in the ring, and we would do it. It was all basic stuff - tackles and slams. We just followed his lead. In the middle of the workout, in walked a guy I would later find out was named "Sweet Daddy" Falcone. He was a big guy, well over six foot tall and a mobster looking 275 pound. He came in with his tag partner and sat down on the couch with Mr. Akbar.

We were taking turns wrestling each other when Alex told me to get in and lock up with him. I did and he proceeded to take me into the corner turnbuckle. He reared back and laid into me with a forearm that didn't seem pulled one bit. After that he pulled his arm back and chopped my chest so hard I didn't know how to react. It stung like nothing else I had ever felt. Just as I was wondering what happened, he lit me up with about three more chops. I was wondering if Mr. Akbar was going to admonish Alex for being so hard on me when I could hear him clap his hands together, chomp his cigar, and yell, "Good, good!"

For the next several minutes Alex slammed me, shot me off the ropes, and laid in some hard hitting elbows. Alex had a great looking kick and he used it; that wasn't bad at all. But when I doubled over to "sell" the move, he clobbered me with some tough forearms to my back. He took me into the corner one more time and lit me up really good with a flurry of chops and forearms and again Skandar Akbar kept cheering him on saying, "Good, good."

The rest of the workout kept that same intensity - hard, physical, and as real as anything had felt all of camp. It was November, but it was warm and the sweat was dripping off me. My chest had started to welt up, and I could see Alex's hand print on it. I knew Ric Flair, Wahoo McDaniel, Greg Valentine, and others all chopped and chopped hard. This was part of the business. If I couldn't handle this, I didn't belong. End of story. He was asking me, "How bad do you want this?" I was being prepared for the ring. What was I going to do when I had a match with a guy who wrestled tight or stiff?

After the workout was over and Mr. Akbar left, Falcone and his partner got in the ring. They were going to do a tag match, a workout. Alex Porteau got in the ring and had Shane be his tag partner. As they were getting ready to start, in walked this guy

47

who hung out at the gym. He sat down next to the rest of us students and was going to watch with us. No, he wasn't. Falcone and Alex asked the guy politely to leave. He said he knew what all this stuff was about, not to worry about it. Falcone and Alex disagreed; they were not going to expose the business in front of this guy, no way. Alex finally said to the rest of us students, "Hey guys, why don't you take off also? No one in the room besides us four."

We all got up and left. I was pissed. I knew I was missing a training opportunity watching these four guys put together a match. It was still a mystery to me how the pros did it. I was annoyed this selfish fucker ruined that chance, but I got up and left.

The drive home after that workout was full of thinking and analyzing. I listened to Bob Segar on I-35 South and thought about the session. When you're starting, one of the hardest things to learn is giving your body openly to your opponent. You have to trust they're not going to hurt you or be a bully. But as I showered and ate in the Super 8 in Temple, I knew even though it was hard and painful Alex never injured me. I was bruised up and sore, but he never hurt me. I had signed up for professional wrestling. I was slowly, painfully learning not everything in the ring could be light. Some things were just going to hurt; there was no way around it. I was going to have to pay some dues.

The next several weeks consisted of me driving seven hours one way to camp and working the other five days at Subway in Eagle Pass. My grandmother was fine with me and my brother Ismael living there, and I had settled into a decent routine.

But I had plenty of time to think when I was driving, and I was getting tired of the long drive to camp. I was thinking of moving somewhere closer to camp - a place I could get a job at and yet live in a town similar in size to Muscatine. Living in a big city was unappealing to me. Since I grew up in a town of 25,000 people in the Midwest with no large city we ever spent time in, I only thought of the negative aspects of big cities - the crime, expensive living, weird people. Nowadays big cities are cleaner. TV shows depict a vibrant life, and they are much safer.

At the time though the images of the LA riots were fresh in my mind. I was also dealing with being homesick, because I couldn't go home easily like when I was living in Nebraska.

I drove past a Hardees in Round Rock on my way to camp near Austin, Texas. I stopped in one day and applied for a job. The owner talked to me and, since there were not many Hardees in Texas and I had experience, he was eager to hire me as a shift manager. He offered me a job if I was interested. I knew the work wouldn't be much fun, but I was familiar with the job. Also, fifteen minutes north was a small town of about 15,000 called Georgetown. It seemed very quiet and safe. I could rent a nice apartment for $400 a month.

So, I proceeded to make what looking back was one of the biggest mistakes of my wrestling journey. If an aspiring actor wants to get anywhere, they move to L.A.,or maybe New York. Imagine instead of that actor moving to L.A., he goes all the way to California, but settles in San Francisco. I had made the bold, gutsy move to leave home. I had found a great camp. I was doing well, and I had found my mentor in Skandar Akbar. I needed to be in Dallas, damn it! But I was too young and stupid to understand that. If you're trying to "make it" in something, you have to be where the action is. Georgetown, Texas, might as well have been Muscatine, Iowa. There were plenty of nice suburbs in the Dallas metro area I could have lived in. Fort Worth, Arlington, and Denton all had plenty of places I could have settled in and been fine while still being half an hour or less from Dallas.

On a trip back home, I told my girlfriend Sarah I was getting an apartment. I said if we were going to stay together, she was going to have to move in with me. What an jerk. Poor Sarah went home and told her parents she was quitting her job and moving to Texas with me. Her parents were not happy, but we pulled away from Muscatine and moved to Georgetown. I knew I cared about Sarah and missed her, but looking back it was also very selfish.

CHAPTER TWELVE
JBL

Camp continued and I was being told I was doing well and progressing. Bad news came though in the news that the Global Wrestling Federation was closing its doors. I knew that was my best chance to get my first match and, though I wasn't ready for it yet, I was getting closer and could see getting a match in a month or two. Skandar Akbar didn't seem too concerned about it as a lot of promoters were bidding for the building, the world famous Sportatorium. One of the names bidding was legendary promoter Jim Crockett.

Crockett had once run the large, profitable Carolina territory. His father started the promotion and Jim ran it since the 70's with it always being a major player in wrestling. As Vince McMahon began his national push in 1984 with the help of cable TV, Jim Crockett seemed to be the only person who had a chance to compete with him. He had the prized TBS two-hour slot on Saturdays from 1985 to 1988. His program was exciting and had featured the best stars of the traditional style of pro wrestling, the NWA. Every week Ric Flair and the four Horseman, Dusty Rhodes, Magnum TA, The Rock & Roll Express, and so much top talent created an incredible two hours of TV. They toured the country, ran PPV events, and it could be argued Jim Crockett was at one time the second most powerful man in wrestling, behind only Vince McMahon.

Crockett eventually did get the Sportatorium and Skandar Akbar would mention at camp meetings he was in the loop with Crockett as they were preparing the new promotion. They ran a few "spot" shows outside of the Sportatorium and the first signs of trouble came up. I heard at the end of camp Alex mention to Akbar to keep him in mind for any new shows. Apparently, Alex wasn't booked on the show. Now I understand that any time you have a new promoter, new coach, or a new manager in any field there are changes. Changes in talent, management, and all kinds of things. The new boss picks his team and sometimes those personnel change. Sometimes people clean house; other times it's more subtle. Regardless, Crockett didn't seem to think Alex was as good of a talent as Global, who had put the light heavyweight title on him multiple times, did.

Sarah and I spent Thanksgiving in Texas both a little homesick. I settled in to my job at Hardees and she got a job at a bakery a block away form our apartment. It helped to be near, because we didn't have a second car, only mine. It couldn't have been easy for her being far away from home stranded without a car until I got home from work.

Christmas time came and we decided to go home for a week. I missed a session of camp and when I came back I was told Alex Porteau was gone. He must have gotten tired of not getting booked in Texas, so he moved. He and his beautiful Puerto Rican wife were expecting. We didn't know this at the time, but Alex had moved to Florida where she had family, I believe. He got a job at an airline eventually.

One of my fellow trainees said I had missed a great session of camp last week though. The new North American Heavyweight champion John Hawk came in and worked out with them. He was coming this week also. He had just defeated Kevin Von Erich for the title and was joining us to train.

A little while later John Hawk came in. He was with James Beard the head referee I had seen on Global TV many times. All I knew about Hawk was what my fellow trainee said. He also mentioned he had played a season of NFL football for the Raiders. I later found out Hawk also played Division 11 football for Abilene Christian. He was trained in Minnesota of all places by Brad Rheingans despite being a native Texan. Rheingans ran an excellent camp and prior to that had been a trainer for Verne Gagne's camp.

Hawk looked to be about six foot six or seven, and weighed around three hundred pounds. He didn't seem to be a bodybuilder, but just a big, rugged, and athletic son of a bitch. He reminded me a lot of Barry Windham. It turned out he was from Sweetwater, Texas, the same hometown Windham was billed from.

I wore glasses at the time and was blind without them. As all of us students were standing around in the ring stretching and talking, I saw my girlfriend Sarah near John Hawk who was butt naked. Not a stitch of clothes. I wasn't sure how to react. I was

52

annoyed, but I really couldn't see what was happening. I also knew that frankly my girlfriend shouldn't have been there. But what the hell was I going to do? Confront this big, tough-looking bastard for undressing in a place there shouldn't be any women at anyway? So, I did the smart thing and shut up.

Hawk paired up with me and said we would have a match against two other students. So, we started. No talking beforehand, no spots called, we just started wrestling. Hawk was obviously in another league. He was powerful and made everything impressive and full of impact. When Hawk locked up with our biggest student John, who was over six foot nine and 350 pounds, everyone was watching. Hawk did things to him we never dreamed of. Suplexes, throws, powerslams all rocked our fellow student John, but he took every shot without complaining.

After the workout with Hawk was over, he thanked us. He said wrestling only once a week in the Main Event at the Sportatorium was tough to do as he got winded. He needed this workout. The rest of us had some more training matches and Hawk actually said, "That little Mexican kid is pretty good."

While we were training, I also heard Beard tell Skandar that John and he were going on a tour of Japan soon. Did Akbar know of any talent that was ready for this? Akbar mentioned someone and then they began talking about the way things were in Japan.

Hawk said the locker room was sacred; the owner of the company wasn't even allowed in the dressing room. Akbar got to talking about his one lone trip to Japan. He mentioned the students they had at the Japanese dojo came out looking like raw meat. I didn't learn until later Akbar was on a famous tour of Japan with Ric Flair, Dusty Rhodes, and Dick Murdoch. The two Texans rode the young Flair hard, hazing him incessantly.

The three got to talking about one of my favorite wrestlers Kerry Von Erich. Kerry was a legend in Texas. With a chiseled body, good looks, and dripping with charisma, he and his brothers set the Dallas territory on fire. Kerry was the biggest box office draw of them all. Hawk talked about a small independent spot show where Kerry sold an ungodly amount of 8x10 photos.

It was great eavesdropping on this conversation, but the workout was over. Before they left, Beard and Hawk talked to us students for over fifteen minutes and answered questions. Hawk talked about the fact heels called a match. He patiently explained how you wrestle a guy bigger then you and how they sell your offense. He compared it to a video game. When you're climbing the different stages of a game to the top, the guys you fight take more and more offense to beat. The same is true with a larger foe. They simply take more offense to chop down.

Beard explained how a guy can carry himself in the ring and appear to be much bigger. Randy Savage was the best example. Savage was barely 200 pounds soaking wet, but how he wrestled and moved in the ring and how he carried himself made him seem so much bigger. I didn't quite understand what Beard meant, but I took note of it as I was going to often be the smaller guy in the ring.

A fellow trainee invited them to have some drinks, but they politely declined.   Hawk said he didn't have much money, and they had to get going.

When Sarah and I were leaving Doug's Gym, I asked her what happened in there when Hawk was undressing. She said right before Hawk took his pants off he turned to her and asked, "Ma'am, would you mind turning away?" A Texas gentleman. Good thing I kept my mouth shut. I would have got my ass kicked for no reason.

IPW Wrestler James Jeffries & James Beard

CHAPTER THIRTEEN

Crockett

Even though we had a great workout with John Hawk, I was still disappointed to hear Alex was gone. Alex seemed to be the kind of wrestler who could show me how to work the fast-paced, high-flying, light heavyweight style I felt I wanted to do. I thought that style best suited me and would help me stand out from the monsters in the business.

As camp continued, we never saw John Hawk again and our training suffered. Mr. Akbar was still there every week, but he was at an age he couldn't get in the ring and work with us. It became more experienced student wrestling less experienced student, but some of us caught a break when Skandar Akbar had Shane and big John come down to the Sportatorium and meet Jim Crockett. They also got to work out before the show in the ring. I had missed Skandar's phone call, so I wasn't able to make it.

The following week Skandar told us three we could all go up there and work out before the show if we wanted. He also told me he would introduce me to Jim Crockett as Mr. Crockett had heard about me from him and wanted to meet me.

I drove up on a Saturday afternoon, I believe, and pulled up to the world famous building I had seen so many times on ESPN. It was such a disappointment! The building looked old, rundown, and so much smaller in person. There were stories of Japanese tourists who would come to Dallas and ask to see two things: the Ewing ranch Southfork made famous by the prime time soap opera "Dallas" and the Sportatorium.

I walked in and saw Bobby Duncam Jr. working out with a guy even smaller than me. The guy was good though and obviously a friend of Duncam's. I saw my friend Shane from camp, and when Duncam was done we got in the ring and worked out.

Sam Houston showed up at ringside and was watching us. Sam was a guy I was very familiar with and excited to meet. I saw him wrestle Ric Flair several times on TBS and have great matches with him. Sam was Jake The Snake's younger brother and the son of Grizzly Smith, a very influential agent for several wrestling companies and a big star in the 60's and 70's.

Sam was generous with his time. He gave us pointers and

wanted to see what we could do. He talked about the fact he could control the crowd with his arm up in the air as well as with a wrestling move. He told stories about old timers such as Tojo Yammamoto who would exaggerate certain gestures to get the crowd into a frenzy. Tojo wouldn't just walk behind his opponent when he had him in a compromising position; he would do an exaggerated walk tippy-toe style with hands thrust up in the air to get the crowd worked up.

Skandar hooked me up with some free tickets for the night's Sportatorium card. We stayed long enough for the first intermission, but didn't see any memorable matches. One featured Manny Villalobos, an aging Hispanic wrestler who didn't have his best outing. Another match had Randy Rhodes, a journeyman wrestler who was doing the gimmick he was Dusty Rhodes' brother. He did look a lot like Rhodes in the face, but didn't have his skills or charisma. I didn't get to see Skandar in action or the Main Event of Tony Norris, the future Ahmed Johnson vs John Hawk.

This night was a perfect example of of why I should have been living in Dallas. We left early, because we had a three-hour drive to Georgetown and work in the morning. I should have been at the Sportatorium every single night they had a card and every afternoon working out and networking with the boys. There was nowhere else I wanted to be more than there. Why wasn't I making it happen?

We had another opportunity to go to the Sportatorium soon after when Jim Crockett held the NWA tag team tournament. They had announced the show the last time I was there, and it was going to be jam-packed with talent.

That afternoon I pulled up to the Sportatorium and found Mr. Akbar right away. He told me to follow him as he was going to introduce me to Jim Crockett. I was starstruck when I saw Robert Gibson as soon as I walked in. He smiled at me, shook my hand, and introduced himself in his southern accent.

Sitting at a desk was Jim Crockett. Next to him was legendary Texas star Dick Murdock. Murdock formed one of the greatest tag teams of all time with Dusty Rhodes in the 70's. He was also a big singles star in every major territory as well as Japan and Puerto Rico. He was sitting next to John Hawk. Both shook my hand.

Next, I introduced myself to Jim Crockett. He was very polite to me and could tell I was nervous. He made small talk about the fact I was from Iowa. Looking back, I don't know this, but he probably only agreed to meet me as a favor to Skandar Akbar. Possibly, he agreed because he needed low-cost talent to work preliminary bouts. I also can't help but think he wanted and needed a young Hispanic wrestler. I spoke Spanish and was hungry for experience. The cards in Dallas and his TV lacked a young Hispanic local wrestler.

I wasn't prepared for this opportunity. I showed up to camp in great shape. But living in Georgetown, I didn't have access to a gym and my workouts suffered. I worked out at home, but I was not in great shape. My hair looked terrible, I had thick glasses Jim Cornette style and I was in desperate need of a makeover. I don't think I made a great impression.

Nonetheless, I headed to the locker room. There Shane and I got dressed to work out. Shane and big John were going to actually have matches on the card. I wasn't jealous; I was happy for them. Shane had been training longer and with his size was ready. John wasn't quite ready I thought, but he was huge! I completely understood why Crockett booked him.

In the locker room was Black Bart. I stayed as far away from Bart as I could, kept my mouth shut, and just generally tried not to make eye contact. Bart wasn't a jerk to me; he just came across as a guy who didn't like young wrestlers. He seemed like he had a temper. He was a veteran, a big guy at around six foot four or so. He looked like he'd be at home in the toughest redneck bar you could ever imagine.

Next walked in Hercules Hernandez all jacked up. I was marking out when he came up and shook my hand enthusiastically wearing a Japanese steakhouse jacket. I had seen Hernandez wrestle Hulk Hogan on Saturday Night's Main Event and on WWF TV for several years.

I couldn't believe the past half hour as Shane and I walked to

59

the ring and began working out. Before we knew it, several more of the wrestlers from the night's card showed up and surrounded the ring. John Hawk was talking to Hector Guerrero about a show they worked together in Mexico. They were having a friendly argument with the Rock & Roll Express over who had the hardest rings - Mexico or the WWF. Robert Gibson came in and helped us out in the ring. He told me I needed to work on my punches, but I was doing okay.

After the workout was over, I made it a point to come up to Hector Guerrero and tell him I really enjoyed watching him wrestle when I was young. I told him I loved watching all the Guerrero's such as Chavo and him. He was very gracious and encouraging to me.

I left the arena and took a nap at the hotel. When I returned to the Sportatorium for the night's card, I was shocked at how small the crowd was. It looked like it was around 200 people! The card was full of incredible talent here in a major city, and this card couldn't draw! Crockett had TV and connections like no one else, but this didn't look good. I remembered John had wrestled his first match ever a couple weeks earlier, in Odessa I think, and it didn't draw well at all either.

Even thought the show didn't draw, it was a good night of wrestling. John Hawk was having a good match when the top rope busted and he flew backwards over it, landed outside the ring, and seemed to be knocked out.

Shane's very first match was under a mask teaming with true journeyman Dusty Wolfe as the Infernos vs The Rock & Roll Express. Shane did well and took the fall for the loss after the double drop kick.

Big John had a terrible night though. He wrestled as the Blue Eagle teaming with Black Bart. I cant remember the team they wrestled, but John messed up quite a bit of his part of the match and Bart seemed pissed.

I knew enough about the business to wonder about what happened next. Keep in mind this was a tag team tournament. Two matches later the ring announcer says they are having a special challenge match. Out comes Black Bart. I had a bad feeling who was coming out next and sure enough it was the Blue Eagle. This didn't look good. When the bell rang, Black Bart proceeded to clothesline, stomp, kick, and pound the hell out of John. After five minutes of pure offense, Bart finally pinned my six foot nine 350 pound friend John.

John didn't go to camp the next week. John never wrestled again, and I never saw him again. I honestly think Bart got pissed at John, demanded a match with him, and piss pounded him in the ring. John took it. I don't judge him for that. What else was he going to do? John walked out of the ring standing. John was a sweet, nice guy and he was tough. He was eager to get in the ring with John Hawk and never complained, but I don't think he was a fan of wrestling. I think he was one of those guys people always come up to and say, "Hey, why don't you try wrestling?" He tried it, and probably got his first couple matches before he was ready. Then he ran into a guy who didn't have the patience to work with him.

It was a different time in the wrestling world, and this is how green new wrestlers were handled. Right or wrong. The Undertaker had one of his first matches with Bruiser Brody under a mask in the Sportatorium and took a pounding, including several chair shots. It is said he went to the dressing room, shook Brody's hand, and thanked him for the match.

CHAPTER FOURTEEN

Leaving Texas

After the tournament, I heard rumblings Crockett's business wasn't doing too well. It wasn't hard to believe with the crowds I'd seen. As I looked at the entire landscape of the business, it was struggling. All the smaller territories were dying or dead. WCW was struggling financially and its quality of wrestling was bad. I'd heard Skandar Akbar say Jim Cornette's exciting Smoky Mountain Wrestling was losing money. I was surprised to hear this since the magazines always raved about its product. Even the WWF was in bad shape and losing money. Japan and Mexico seemed to be the only places thriving, but getting booked there was something that didn't happen right away. It took some seasoning first. I needed to get booked in Texas first before I could make some connections to Mexico. Many of the wrestlers such as John Hawk wrestled in the northern states of Mexico.

Looking back, it was the worst time I've ever seen in the wrestling business. 1994 and 1995 are documented as terrible years for the industry. A variety of factors caused this such as a steroid scandal that forced Hulk Hogan to the sidelines. Vince McMahon went on trial for selling steroids and had to take his attention away from his company. Older stars faded away without any new ones to replace them.

All this was bad news for me. If Jim Crockett went out of business, where was I going to get my first match? I didn't have any connections and Skandar was my only hope.

I kept attending camp, but it seemed like nothing was happening. We didn't have a trainer, and I wasn't really learning anything new. I was ready for my first match so I could start learning some more. I knew I had to get in the ring with people better than me. I had to start having matches.

Eventually, it became apparent Crockett was done with the Sportatorium and wrestling for good. It was kind of frightening to me that the man who once employed Ric Flair couldn't make this successful. He had TV, talent, tons of experience, and he couldn't continue.

March turned to April with still nothing, no first match. By May, Sarah and I had decided we shouldn't stay any longer. I was bleeding money, and nothing was happening. I told Mr. Akbar I was going home. I told him I didn't want to quit this, but I didn't see anything changing. "You're not going to quit," he told me. He said it wasn't like the old days where he could call someone and get me booked. He had tried, but there weren't many shows being run.

So, I packed my car up and headed back home. I wondered if I ever was going to have a match. Was I ever going to be a wrestler? All my life people thought my dream was a bit crazy. I always knew it was going to be difficult, but I'd found a good camp and was doing well. Skandar and many of the people who came in to visit the school said I was ready for my first match, but I couldn't seem to make it happen. I'd come so far only to come up short again.

CHAPTER FIFTEEN

Back to Iowa

When I went back home, I got a job again at Hardees on the South end. I got hired as an assistant manager making $350 a week salary. The money was okay and the work was fine. My old co-worker Alan sang "Welcome Back" from the old 70's TV series when I walked back in. I didn't feel very good about myself coming back to the old restaurant, but I didn't have a lot of choice.

I kept in touch with Skandar over the phone, occasionally calling. He was always nice and had time for me. Nothing was changing in Texas he told me.

I kept my routine up trying to whittle my debt down that I had accumulated in Texas. Sarah and I had an apartment near downtown. One day, I was talking to a friend of mine who was going through a divorce and lost his mobile home. I asked him what was going to happen to it. He said he didn't know, but I could contact the financing company. "Buy it. No hard feelings," he said. After dealing with a few frozen pipes, I bought it for $3,000. Consolidating my credit card debt I racked up in Texas with the $3,000 helped me start paying off my bills.

I began to make it a weekly routine to call Skandar Akbar. I wanted to keep myself in the loop on the happenings in Texas and not let him forget about me. Some weeks were easy to call him; other weeks I felt like an annoying telemarketer. It seemed like the only thing I could do was to keep my dreams on life support. I vividly remember one summer night calling him and he was noticeably down. I asked him what was the matter and he said, "Ah, Juan, we lost Dick Murdock today." Skandar had gone way back with Murdock and, like so many of Murdock's contemporaries, he took it hard.

One day Skandar said some new owners had opened the Sportatorium back up. That was good to hear even though I was far away. Turned out Skandar Akbar was a part of the front office. The main guy handling things was Grizzly Smith. Grizzly was Cowboy Bill Watts right hand man of wrestling operations for years in Mid-South. I had also seen Grizzly Smith on WCW television as an agent. Basically in those two roles Grizzly handled the arena shows, helped with TV tapings, kept the wrestlers under control, and helped younger wrestlers with their matches.

Their was another person handling the booking. Even though Skandar had influence, he didn't make final decisions. He was basically a manager as talent in the ring and an adviser and sounding board in the office. However, it was still promising.

After one of my weekly calls, Skandar said he thought I might be booked! He talked to me the next week and gave me a date. Things were looking up when he called about two weeks before the match and said I got scratched; I was off the card. I was so disappointed.

I was feeling sorry for myself when I snapped out of it. I had already asked for the three days off. I had enough money to drive to Dallas and pay for a couple cheap hotel rooms. Why not go to the Sportatorium? There was nowhere else I'd rather be. The cost was manageable and I could maybe get to work out with someone and meet some of the office. I asked Skandar what he thought. He said it'd be a good idea and I was welcome to be there.   It'd be good for me to meet Grizzly.

I drove fifteen hours one way to try to get a foot in the door again. When I walked in to the Sportatorium in the late morning, Grizzly Smith was there. He asked me if I was Skandar's boy and I said yes. He invited me to hang out wherever I'd like. I went to the locker room and then the ring, but no one was there yet.

I walked into the office where Grizzly was at and he told me to have a seat and I was welcome to join him. I wasn't going to turn that down. I was always fascinated by Mid-South Wrestling. Great talent and so many great angles came out of that territory. I always wanted to work for Bill Watts, because that seemed to be the place people made the jump from wrestler to star. I had so many things I wanted to ask Grizzly, but I also wanted to make sure I wasn't intruding on his business or work.

Grizzly made me feel right at home. Soon after we got to talking, Skandar Akbar walked in with Burger King for him and Grizzly. Sitting with those two that afternoon was a lesson in old school wrestling and nostalgia. Grizzly told me about what made his son Jake "The Snake" Roberts such a great wrestler. He talked about how Jake refereed a few matches as he was starting in order to get his feet wet.

Grizzly and Ak talked about a wrestler who had heat with the promoter, so the promoter booked a boxer vs wrestler match. He paid the boxer, an ex world champion, extra money to give this unsuspecting wrestler a beating.

Ak told a story of driving with Pat O'Connor, the former world heavyweight champion in the Omaha area. O'Connor got a speeding ticket.   The police officer recognized him and asked for an autograph. The ex champ did one better and took out several pictures and signed one for each of the officer's kids. The last thing the officer did was thank O'Connor as he handed him his ticket!

This went on for hours. Stories shared about Watts, booking philosophies, and how sex sells in wrestling. I just sat there soaking it all in. I was just glad I was there to sit under the learning tree. Skandar also told me Alex Porteau would be wrestling tonight. Turned out Alex had moved to Florida and got a job at an airline. One of the perks of the job was he got to fly for little or no money. So, he was getting booked regularly in Dallas again. Also, Ak told me Charlie Norris from Minnesota would be teaming with Sam Houston for the first time. Charlie was a big six foot six Native American who had wrestled for WCW for about a year. He started in Minnesota and could maybe get me some contacts that could get me booked there.

After some time passed, I got changed and went to the ring. No one was there so I hit the ropes, did my Rocky Brewer somersaults, and took some bumps. After a while in walked Sweet Daddy Falcone. He asked someone at the building if Hart's boy was training today.   I assumed that meant Gary Hart's son. He had two guys I had seen in the front row at shows before with him The CWA, the name of the new promotion, had a training camp and these two guys signed up. They were just starting and didn't have much athletic ability, but beyond that I don't know what happened to them. I watched Falcone lead them through some drills, demonstrated a hip toss, and show a few other small moves.

I headed out of the ring as it appeared no one was going to be doing anything else. In the locker room after I changed, I met Charlie Norris. Charlie was very cordial to me and told me I only needed to know one name really. He gave me the phone number of Eddie Sharkey. Sharkey had trained Charlie, ran shows, and still had a camp. He had trained a large number of wrestlers in the 80's who went on to be big stars. The Road Warriors, Rick Rude, Demolition Smash, and many others came out of his camp.

After that I headed outside to get some fresh air. I also knew there was a strict rule for greenhorns like me. If you weren't booked, you weren't in the locker room as bell time got close. I saw a car pull up and out of the passenger seat walked out Alex Porteau! I was so happy to see my old trainer and glad he remembered me. Alex looked great. I will always remember the impression Alex made that day. He looked fit and athletic. He was well dressed with Khakis and a polo shirt. He had his bag with him, because he just got picked up from DFW airport. He looked like a professional. He looked like a wrestler.

Alex told me about the fact he just had a tryout with the WWE and it went well. He had a match with Goldust. He was hopeful the tryout would lead to something.

As I hung out at my car, I saw Charlie Norris walk to the liquor store across the street from the Sportatorium with a brown bag. I got my comp tickets, entered the arena as a fan, and watched a group of professionals put on a great card. I couldn't believe that was the first time Charlie was wrestling in Texas as the tag match against Falcone and his partner was fantastic. How could these guys get in there and have a great match that had the crowd enthralled without working together before? Alex had a great match. In the main event, "Firebreaker" Chip was the headliner.

After the match I got to the back and said goodbye to Skandar and Grizzly. In the locker room, Chip talked a little with me. He told me he was a business owner in the Mid Atlantic area and just was coming to Dallas to help the promotion out. He talked like he was phasing himself out of wrestling. He worked in WCW for a while and was still in great shape. He told me as I was leaving,

"Well, if you got trained by Alex and Ak, you at least got some good training." He was right. I wasn't always grateful for the experience I had at camp at that stage in my life. I was frustrated with being unable to secure my first match, but slowly I was getting educated. Everyone loved and respected Ak. He was great with young wrestlers.

When I drove home, I was glad I made the trip. Nothing concrete came of it, and I didn't even have much of a workout. However, I had a great time, got my face seen, and made a promising contact with Charlie. I sat under the learning tree of Grizzly and Ak.

When I got home, I called Eddie Sharkey and he told me Charlie talked to him about me. Charlie told him I looked good and lived in Iowa. Eddie sounded like he would book me, but nothing ever came of it.

One night while I was watching Monday night Raw from San Antonio leading up to the Shawn Michaels vs Bret Hart Wrestlemania match, I saw Alex Porteau wrestling in a tag match against The Godwins. Soon after his tryout match with Goldust, he got hired by the WWF and became "The Pug." Alex never had a Hall of Fame career in WWF but he made it to the big time. He worked an overseas tour and wrestled opening match against John Hawk at Madison Square Garden. He's still wrestling today and I'm proud to say I was trained by him.

I was making my weekly calls with Skandar over the next few months when one day he called *me* and left a message on my machine. I phoned him right away. He called to tell me that I was booked at the Sportatorium, and this time I wouldn't get scratched.

It was finally going to happen. I was going to have my first wrestling match.

CHAPTER SIXTEEN

First Match

I packed up my boots and my bags and headed back south down I-35. I took several days off for the drive and to arrive there Wednesday night to work out in Doug's Gym at Skandar's school. After my workout I woke up to find myself in terrible pain from not having bumped in a ring for a while, let alone a stiff, hard ring. I took the next day easy with laying in the hotel bed and only venturing out for the Denny's next door.

I arrived Friday at the Sportatoruim early as usual. I ran into Grizzly Smith and Skandar Akbar right away. I sat down with them again for an hour or so.

I had brought a gift this time. When I was back home, I got to thinking about a book my local bookstore had. It was called *Friday Night at the Coliseum*. It detailed the local wrestling scene in Houston with some great old black and white photos packaged in a coffee-style book. I had checked the book out a dozen times over the years at my library and had forgotten about it. But I got to thinking that maybe it had a photo of Skandar Akbar in it. It did. It had two great pictures of Akbar from the mid to late 60's. One picture was him in his robe and another was of him pushing away from a lock up. It also had a picture of Bronco Lubich, an old friend of Ak and a longtime referee of the old World Class promotion.

Ak and Grizzly looked through the book and their eyes seemed to board a time machine full of old friends, camaraderie, and people who had passed on. The pictures uncovered a time when they were all young and strong doing what they loved to do in an era that was long gone. Mil Mascaras, Wahoo McDaniel, and all the stars of the Houston Wrestling promotion ran by Paul Bosch were in there.

I told Mr. Akbar he could have it. I decided I would pay the twenty dollars to give my trainer and mentor this rare book. I don't think he had ever seen it, let alone owned it. He had a big smile when he showed it to the boys who started filing in such as Action Jackson, a black, area wrestler who was big and experienced. Jackson asked him if he remembered the match that was pictured and Ak said he did. He said the days were more fun then,and he told Jackson, "There was more camaraderie."

Grizzly told me I'd be wrestling second match with my opponent being Scott Braddock. I didn't know who he was, and they didn't tell me anything else about what to expect.

I went into the locker room and got changed to work out. A guy who used to go to Doug's toward the end of my time there was also there to work out. We went into the ring. We had about a forty-five minute workout. When I told him who I was wrestling, he said the guy was a good worker.

I went into the locker room and just waited. Keep in mind that in the entire time I had been training no one had ever explained to me how a match actually happened. Who gets to win? How long do you wrestle? Is it fixed? I realize to current fans and wrestlers it seems hard to believe, but I had never been told by Skandar, Alex, Grizzly, anyone at all that the business was a work! I still was in the dark, and that is how they wanted it to be. I still wasn't part of the fraternity.

Little by little the guys from the card began to file in shaking everyone's hand, even mine. A few of the guys I had already met like Sam Houston and Falcone, but others I hadn't. Scott Putski, the son of "Polish Power" Ivan Putski, was the current CWA champion and was there headlining the card. Putski was a former Division 1 football player at Texas Christian University. He stood about my height, had a powerful frame, and looked ready to make the move to the next level. He was very nice to me, and talked to me about growing up a second generation wrestler, dealing with Polish jokes growing up, and his football days.

I asked him if he had worked in Mexico before, and he said he had many times. He shocked me when he told me it was a beautiful country, and he wouldn't mind living there actually. All I had seen in my summers visiting family was the border and it didn't look too beautiful to me. Here was a Polish guy telling a Mexican guy that Mexico was a great place to live!

Finally, Scott Braddock walked in and I stood up and shook his hand. He was a legit 250 pounds of muscle. He had a beard, a large frame, and looked like he dead-lifted for a living. He was cordial to me as I let him know this was my first match, and I was willing to do whatever he wanted to do. We sat near each other and I finally asked him how it all worked. Who was going to give us direction? He said not to worry about it, Grizzly and the booker Johnny Mantell would give us instructions on how long we would go. I always had dreams of winning my first match when I was a teenager. But now standing in this locker room with this experienced grown man who had about forty to fifty pounds on me, I had absolutely no qualms about losing my first match.

I found out later Scott had wrestled for World Class in its dying days and tagged frequently with a couple future mega stars by the names of Cactus Jack and Steve Austin, winning the belts with Cactus. He had worked that area for several years and was respected as a good hand. Maybe he was not a classical wrestler, but he was still a good wrestler who could have a match with a green as shit rookie like me.

Sure enough, I saw the referee James Beard walk into the locker room and signal the first match to the office. In the office were Skandar, Grizzly, and booker Johnny Mantell. We were next, and there for the very first time I was was told how it would work. Grizzly told Braddock he wanted him to go over, but to make sure he let me do a few things. He said, "Don't eat him up. I want to see what he can do, Scott." Braddock nodded respectfully and then Grizzly told him to keep it in the ring and go around ten minutes. If I was in the room you wouldn't have known it, no one talked to me. Honestly, there wasn't anything wrong with that. I was the dumb shit in the room and they were the guys with almost one hundred fifty years combined experience doing this.

Beard asked Braddock what the finisher was and Braddock said neck breaker. One of the wrestlers in the room walked in and asked Braddock why he did what he did last week. "I had big plans for that kid! I was going to make him a star, and then you go and break his neck with that damn finisher of yours! Damn it, be more careful next time will you!" I was pretty sure I was being ribbed. I didn't get the sense Braddock would be that type of guy, but having seen what happened to Big John I made sure everyone was smirking about the joke.

We went back to the locker room and got ready. The ring announcer came up and asked for my weight and hometown. I asked him if I could could be announced as Latin Thunder along with my name and he said sure. When you read Mick Foley's book, he writes that Dallas helped him enjoy the sport again after he was so miserable in Memphis. I don't know why but Dallas just was a great place to be a young, aspiring wrestler. The veterans helped you as long as you respected the business and wanted to learn. Whenever I opened my mouth to ask a question after wondering if it was okay, I always got an answer with a patient explanation. Never bullying, never belittling. Little things like the ring announcer's response all the way up to the top wrestlers and the office made you feel welcome.

Soon I could hear the crowd rustling outside. Before I knew it, the ring announcer started to welcome people and made a few announcements. The first roars of the crowd were so foreign, so unique. As the guys in the first match lined up to get ready, I knew I had to get on deck as soon as they went out. It was one of the rules posted in the locker room. When the National Anthem was played, I knew I was getting close.

Sure enough the announcer's voice boomed over the sound system and the first guys walked out with their security escort. I began to do push ups trying to warm up while trying to calm my frantic nerves. Here I was getting ready to walk out for this moment I'd been waiting for my whole life. This was the Sportatorium! "Get ready," I told myself. I was going to walk down the same aisle Lou Thesz, Harley Race, Ric Flair, and every other star the wrestling business had.

Bam! I heard the first slam of the match before us and the crowds reaction threw my nerves up another notch. They had the crowd going and were doing their job. Before I knew it, I heard another big reaction from the crowd, the bell, and then a loud pop. It was time!

I saw the guys come back from the ring sweating and breathing hard and then Scott Braddock's massive frame being led away by security. As he walked out, I heard boos from the audience. Soon enough my security escort told me, "You're up."

I walked out down the Sportatorium's aisle, a downward slope. In the center of the arena stood the ring under the bright spotlights. The rest of the arena was dark. I was surprised and caught completely off guard when I saw fans from the stands especially kids hold their hands out wanting me to slap them the way I held mine out for "Mr. USA" Tony Atlas twenty years before. It was the only surreal moment I had ever had in my young life.

I promptly screwed up as James Beard directed me to the "good guys" side, but confused I entered the ring from the "bad guys". I shook off the mistake and stood in the ring under those glaring lights ready for my moment nerves still shot.

The bell rang and I circled the ring and locked up with the beast Braddock. Every veteran will tell you you can tell a lot by how someone locks up. Locking up with this powerful man let me know he was going to take care of me. He locked up tight, but loosened up right away. He pushed me to the ropes and, when Beard called for the break, he reared back as far as his arm could go and chopped me hard on the chest. It hurt like hell, so selling the move was not difficult. We locked up again and the same thing happened. A hard stiff chop followed that blistered my chest red.

The third time we locked up I got a lesson in wrestling psychology that I'd been told over and over but didn't understand till that moment. Braddock reared back to chop me again and I blocked it and fired up with a punch that he sold like I was his equal. The crowd roared. One punch, properly set up, that's all it took to get the crowd behind me.

We wrestled the next ten minutes with me getting lost at one point. I wasn't sure what to do next and fired up on Braddock and he let me shoot him off, when I called a dropkick he did what made sense in that point in the match. He let me drop like a sack of potatoes while he held the ropes. The crowd sympathized with me. Braddock told Beard, "He fucked up." I had. He put the boots to me some and got his heat with the crowd. Sensing I was getting eaten up and losing the crowd while Braddock had his back to me, James Beard threw me a spot. "Schoolboy," he whispered as he leaned in to check on my condition. It was perfect. I rolled up Braddock for a pin and the crowd popped as Beard counted to two before Braddock kicked out and regained control.

I was starting to lose the crowd as they weren't believing this green guy they'd never seen before had any hopes of beating Braddock. Braddock whispered to me, "Let's go home." I was relieved. My wind was shot and I had lost the crowd. This wasn't the Apollo Theater in Harlem, but the crowd at the Sportatorium had seen wrestling for decades and they weren't above booing a bad wrestler and I was pushing it.

Braddock got me in position and hit me with his neck breaker. He gently pulled back to snap my neck for effect and he didn't hurt me a bit. I heard Beard count one, two, three! The bell rang and it was over. I was relieved.

I walked to the back a bit disappointed by my performance. When I got back, Braddock said I did okay for my first match. I just screwed up one part of the match. I didn't get to show a lot of offense, but it was a hell of a learning experience, an eye opener. It honestly wasn't anything like camp.

I got changed quietly and talked a bit with Larry Greene, who had been trained by Killer Brooks and wrestled the opener. He asked me if I was alright and I said yes. I just was disappointed by my performance.

After getting dressed, I saw Steve Cox in the back area warming up. He was facing Putski in the Main and looked like a tough, high-caliber athlete. Turned out Cox was a top athlete as he'd played football at The University of Tulsa where he was a team captain. He was in great shape with good size and height. He told me I looked like a Guerrero and proceeded to talk about working out in their ring in the back yard.

I went to the "crows nest" where you could see the matches in a hidden spot where the fans couldn't see us through the glass. I saw all the matches I could. Sitting up there made me realize I had a lot to learn. These guys all had more experience then me. They were almost all in good shape and bigger than me. They had something else I couldn't put my finger on or explain.

Frankly, I looked, wrestled, and acted like a preliminary wrestler.

As the main event came up, Skandar and Grizzly walked into the crows nest to watch. Grizzly noted the crowd had thinned out some. As the match started, Grizzly stated Putski better be careful with Steve Cox saying, "He gives receipts." The match was good with both guys looking like they belonged in the main. Cox won with a side Russian leg sweep and captured the belt.

I hung around for a little while and wondered about whether I should just leave. I wasn't sure if I was going to be paid, since it was never discussed. I decided to say goodbye to the office and thank them for the opportunity. When I walked in, Grizzly handed me an envelope. He told me to count it and confirm it was the amount on a piece of paper he pointed to. I took the envelope and stood there like a dumb ass and looked at Skandar. He repeated exactly what Grizzly had said, so I counted out $40 and signed where they told me. I shook everyone's hands and said goodbye.

As I was gathering my stuff in the office, in walked Sam Houston and Charlie Norris. They got their envelopes and counted them, I thought it was $175, maybe $200 each for the semi main event. I figured the house was around 900 people, but I'm not sure. I knew they had worked the night before in Louisiana and were working again tomorrow, so it was decent money. Things had gotten better than the Crockett days here in Texas.

I walked out of the Sportatorium still a bit down about my match. As soon as I opened the door, the fifty fans or so who were waiting outside for the wrestlers cheered me. It warmed my heart and sincerely lifted my spirits. They knew I was a new, young wrestler and they thought I'd tried hard. Losing your first match was no sin to them. It really made me feel better as I got into my car and headed north.

I drove until I was in Oklahoma and got a room. I grabbed a bite to eat and took a hot shower. I sat down on the bed and thought about what I'd just accomplished. I thought about what it meant to me and how long it took to finally have that first match. I began to cry.

CHAPTER SEVENTEEN

Power Plant

Back home I wasn't sure what do do next. I didn't have a good enough performance to warrant the CWA to feel I was going to help them in any way. I wasn't any closer to discovering these wrestling shows, spot shows I'd heard about. So, I waited for something to happen.

Nothing happened for me. Yet, the industry as a whole was gaining momentum. New stars in WWF were starting to gain traction such as Mankind and Steve Austin. Guys who hadn't been featured in Main Events were coming into their own like Shawn Michaels, Brett Hart, and others. Promising, fresh young faces such as Dwayne Johnson and Hunter Hurst Helmsley were receiving opportunities.

In WCW, they signed up ex WWF stars such as Hulk Hogan, Randy Savage, and many other veterans. These guys were past their prime, but still were at an age when they had some good years left. They also still had the experience and charisma to know how to get over with fans. But WCW's big break was when they signed Kevin Nash and Scott Hall and began an angle that caught fire, the nWo (New World Order).

As I sat at home and watched the sport go from the absolute dumps in 1994/1995 to begin to crack the pop culture of the U.S., I wanted to get my wrestling career on track.

One night while watching WCW, I saw their advertisement for their Power Plant training school. I saw a couple exposes on national TV featuring their brutal initiation. They had a tryout that involved endless Hindu squats using just your bodyweight. In every expose, I saw countless wannabees and great athletes alike dropping out from exhaustion.

I knew I wasn't geared for this type of training or school, but I didn't see anything else out there. I felt that I had to give it a shot. Besides, WCW was a thriving company. If I could get through the school and offered the chance to have some experience against all the veterans they had, it'd be worth it.

I sent for information and received the application in the mail. I gave my notice at Hardees knowing they were not going to offer my job back if this didn't work out. I convinced myself I would just train to be able to do hundreds of free squats and get in great cardiovascular conditioning. For the next three months, I did just that. I spent a lot of time hitting the weights, swimming, and running to improve my wind. I got to the point I could do a hundred free squats without stopping and sets of fifty to sixty with breaks in between easily.

I sold my trailer for a small profit. Once again I dropped everything and headed to Atlanta, Georgia, for my three-day tryout at the infamous Power Plant.

It was a disaster. "Sarge" Dwayne Bruce, the trainer there, got me to quit in less than a day. We started with free squats. Immediately it was followed by up downs. Immediately followed by push ups. Immediately followed by more squats and more up downs. I wasn't ready for this. As a camera crew from HBO Sports followed me to the parking lot, I quit.

It was embarrassing. It was humiliating. I knew this type of camp was not for me from the beginning, but I was so desperate for a chance to get back into wrestling I risked it. I trained hard for it, but I wasn't able to complete the first day.

I've since learned a lot of great talent had the same fate as me. Even Wrestlemania Main Eventer Batista had a bad experience there. But at that time, it was as low as I'd felt in a long time.

CHAPTER EIGHTEEN

Discovering the Indy's

So, back to square one in Muscatine again I decided to get a job at Schwans, that yellow ice cream frozen food company you see delivering food to your neighbors. The hours were brutal. Twelve to fourteen hour days five days a week.

They sent me to Oskaloosa, Iowa, to train. Out of all the places I expected to catch a break in wrestling this was the last. I was taking my CDL driving test one afternoon with a fellow trainee named Ron Finley. Ron was from the blue collar town of Ottumwa where Tom Arnold was from. Ron was your typical working class guy who stood six foot tall with a decent build, but not a gym guy.

After we both promptly flunked our CDL test so badly that we didn't even get to start our trucks, we chatted for a bit. Ron told me he drove with someone who told him I was a pro wrestler. I shrugged it off and explained I went to wrestling school and had my first match in Dallas, but I didn't know if that made me a wrestler.

Ron told me he was a wrestler. "What do you mean?" I asked. Ron explained that he wrestled for a group out of Kahoka, Missouri. They were backyard wrestlers basically, but they had an actual ring and held cards occasionally. Ron asked me if I'd like to go down and train with him one weekend.

I said sure. I wasn't expecting any great wrestler to be down there, but I had nothing going for me so why not.

The next Saturday, Ron and I met at Kahoka. The wrestling I found there was what I expected. No one was a trained wrestler, but there were a few guys I saw who wanted to learn and had some athletic ability and talent. Matt Murphy, a future wrestler, was there. Matt was the only one I had come up and talk about wanting to get trained. He had looked into some schools in the Mid Atlantic region and Matt had some talent.

I told Ron I couldn't train him since I was not really a pro yet myself, let alone qualified to train someone. However, I did tell him I would work out with him and share what I knew with him. Ron was very hungry to get in the business and wanted to learn about it. He was also enthusiastic about it, not as down as I was about the prospects of finding shows to get on. It was great to talk to him on the phone and have someone who I could be friends with. Here was someone my age that I could talk to wrestling about; we helped each other out and I was grateful we had met.

One day after our workouts in Missouri, Ron told me he had a flyer he wanted me to see. It was an advertisement for a wrestling show in Missouri the following weekend. It had a slew of independent wrestlers neither of us had heard of. It had the headliner being an older looking wrestler we'd never heard of named "The Professional." We agreed to go to the show that afternoon on a Sunday to meet the promoter. We would bring my program from my match at the Sportatorium and try to get booked, hopefully against each other.

That next Sunday Ron and I saw the show with our girlfriends and studied it like a test. Some of the wrestlers on the card like James "The Bear" Grizzly were very good and were in great shape. Others had bad physiques and didn't wrestle as good as we did even with our limited experience. Some we felt we were comparable to in skills.

After the show was over, we hung around and talked to someone about meeting the promoter. He went and got the veteran headliner "The Professional," Dan Burdick. Burdick was a bit skeptical, but he talked to us. He looked at my program and at me, not sure if I really was the guy who wrestled the second match on this program.

After a bit, he told us we could get in the ring and show him something. Ron and I locked up in the ring and did a very basic set of spots that lasted about three minutes. Burdick said that was enough. We stepped out of the ring and Burdick took our names. He said we looked a little tight in there, but he would keep us in mind. He didn't run shows all the time, but he had a few planned coming up. He didn't seem too enthusiastic, but we were still glad we made the trip. It was a small window that had opened up and with some luck something would come out of it.

A couple weeks later I got off work at my new job at Bandag, the same company Dad had spent decades at. I had gotten on as a temp at the retread plant working second shift at a different plant than Dad. It paid nine bucks an hour and had some overtime. It was hot work, a little heavy, but nothing backbreaking.

I got a phone call from a wrestler who worked on the card Burdick put on. He was around forty and heavy set, but seemed like he had some experience.

He told me he had a show coming up Friday in Waterloo, Iowa, at a bowling alley. He needed a match to finish out the card. Did I think I could have a decent match with my friend I brought down? I told him we had worked out several times and I was confident we could have a good match despite our inexperience. He asked me if I could make the date on Friday. I said we would, because I knew Ron would do anything necessary to get that day off work. He told me we were booked. The pay was thirty-five dollars each plus gas money.

I called Ron and told him the news. The only person who would have been more excited than me was him. I was interested to see what wrestlers would make up the card and where they got trained. I also was hoping I could find out where they wrestled at in the Midwest, so I could try to get known by promoters.

When Ron and I showed up, the world of independent wrestling in the Midwest I'd been looking for opened up. I met young wrestlers fresh out of camp who I developed friendships and relationships with for decades. Travis Shillington and "Mr. Destiny" Jay Hannah had been trained by Brad Rheingans in Minnesota. I also met James Grizzly who had been on the card in Missouri we had seen. Griz was also a student of Rheingans. "Wicked" Lester Brody who's real name was Cory Welmesley was there. Cory went on to enter the world of MMA and even had a fight for the UFC in Vegas on the under card of a PPV.

Ron and I mingled, introduced ourselves, and talked to anyone we could. Everyone was nice to us. They didn't know what to make of us, since we hadn't been seen or heard of in any of the locker rooms or schools they had attended. I understood why some people were skeptical of us and whether we belonged in the ring or if my credentials of training with Skandar Akbar were legitimate.

Ron and I wrestled in the second or third match. The ring was a hard boxing ring and we actually broke a part of it doing a power bomb. We were eager to impress and we went out and did the classic rookie mistake of too much too soon on the card. The ring ropes were very loose and that hurt me trying to do my high flying spots. It certainly wasn't a great match. We had a much better match earlier in the year and in practice. I thought I'd made Ron look great, but he didn't make me look too good. But a lot of that was the ring and our nerves. I think we still let people know we were legitimate even if we were green.

After the show, we got a few phone numbers and our pay and headed home. It was a huge first step to getting work in the Indy scene. I can honestly say I owed all that to Ron Finley. His enthusiasm and eagerness to search out shows made this happen. The door was open. Now, I had to go through it and see if I could get some work.

CHAPTER NINETEEN

Sam Houston & One Man Gang

A month or so later in the early summer of 1998 Ron and I were booked by "The Professional" Dan Burdick on a card in Missouri. It was a valuable experience. Here was a great chance to have another match with Ron in front of a small live crowd. I talked as much as I could with Griz in the back, since he seemed to be well connected in Minnesota having been trained there. He also stayed busy in Missouri and Kansas, because he lived in the

Kansas City area. Griz was a great wrestler who was in good shape, talented, and a good-looking, biracial, black guy who was as strong as anyone I'd ever been in the ring with.

Ron and I also drove up to Algona, Iowa, to work out with Travis Shillington. He had his very own ring that he constructed in a warehouse. Trav would work out there with his buddy Kenny "Backwash". After meeting some talented area wrestlers and seeing Travis had a ring, I began to think about fulfilling a longtime dream most aspiring wrestlers have. I wanted to wrestle in my hometown. I always thought Muscatine was a good wrestling town. Blue collar and decent-sized, I thought it would also be excited to see live pro wrestling after many years without it. I also thought I'd try something new for Muscatine and use my connections with Skandar to book a name wrestler.

Sure enough, Skandar gave me the number of Sam Houston in Texas. I thought maybe Sam might be willing to make the long drive up here. I also hoped Charlie would as I had heard he was back living in Minnesota. Sam called me right back and said he and Charlie could come up for $200 each plus transportation. That sounded pretty reasonable as a lot of Indy wrestlers with a few matches under their belt could make between $75 and $100.

Sam suggested if I wanted a big name I book The One Man Gang. Gang was a big name in wrestling. He had just finished up a run in WCW where he held the U.S. title before dropping it to Konan. Prior to that he worked in the WWF as Akeem the African Dream. He had been a big star in the Mid-South and World Class territories also. Sam mentioned he had teamed with Charlie against Gang and a Minnesota wrestler named The Hater several times and they had good matches. Despite the terrible name of The Hater, everything else sounded great.

I called Gang and he couldn't have been easier to deal with. His real name being George Gray he was a soft-spoken gentleman who lived in Shreveport, Louisiana. He was a professional all the way offering to fly in on Friday, so he wouldn't be rushed or have a flight delay ruin the show. Gang said his rate was $350 plus a plane ticket. That sounded reasonable also so I booked him. I had a main event I could sell with two names wrestling fans would be excited about.

I was excited about picking up Gang at the Moline airport and talking to him about his career. I learned he started out in the outlaw promotion for Randy Poffo. He told me about how Ernie Ladd got him into Mid-South wrestling. He did some run ins on the Junkyard Dog where he would come in and destroy dog before leaving just as quickly as he came in. He told me Watts was the one who gave him the name after one of the run ins saying in the announcing booth, "This guy is like a One Man Gang!" He said working the Junkyard Dog in downtown New Orleans in front of the rabid black fans who loved Dog was dangerous for your wellbeing. Gang said his wife would put him in the trunk of his car and drive him out of the arena.

Gang told me more stories about my favorite promoter Watts. He said Watts was a great payoff guy who had an incredible mind. He said it wasn't unusual to be on a card where they had three or four hot angles going on. Mid-South seemed to be his favorite promotion.

Gang shared stories of working the WWF against Hulk Hogan. He had several matches with Hogan and spoke highly of him. Gang said Hogan would ask every time if it was okay if they could finish with the leg drop as though anyone was going to suggest anything else. Gang shared that even though Hogan had his own dressing room he would make it a point to go into the boys locker room and shake everyone's hands and spend time with them.

Gang had hopes he might get a WWF contract as he had a couple matches with them that summer. He said everything went well and he had a meeting with Jim Ross, but nothing had happened. He had lost some weight recently and with natural aging he didn't look as menacing as he did in his prime when he was over four hundred pounds and moved like a cat. He thought that might have hurt him some.

On the night of the show, Gang showed up early and signed every autograph and took every picture he was asked to. He watched every match from the back and offered advice to anyone that asked and even a few who didn't. He was a class act.

The show didn't draw too well with about one hundred fifty fans. The biggest problem being I picked a terrible time to run a show - August 31st. The end of the month isn't a great time to run a show. School starting is not a good time either. Neither are warm months. Still, the show was a good chance for me to book a show, learn a lot, and make even more contacts. The quality of the show was good with an outstanding main event. We filled out the rest of the card with good Midwest talent such as Travis and Griz.

I wrestled Ron and we had our best match. It was great to wrestle in my hometown in front of friends and family. It was a stressful night though since we didn't draw that well and I had to take some personal money out to pay everyone. I shorted Ron that night, and I shouldn't have. I had every intention to send him money in the mail and I did that next pay week. However, I shouldn't have taken advantage of his friendship like that.

Legendary trainer Eddie Sharkey came down and refereed the card. He told me he'd make sure he booked me soon. That's how the business worked he said. I never got a call or a booking from Eddie. That was just Eddie Sharkey.

CHAPTER TWENTY

Lenny Lane

After a summer of progress, I got a booking or two before I decided to run another show. I thought if I cut our expenses and changed a few things like ran our own concessions we might be able to turn a profit. Also, I hoped running in December would help significantly. Wrestling in general was getting super hot at this time with the Monday Night Wars between WWF & WCW.

In order to cut travel expenses, I decided to look a little closer to home for our main event. Lenny Lane was a WCW wrestler who appeared on Monday Nitro regularly. Lenny was involved in a small angle with Chris Jericho and was appearing on TV on a show that was drawing record ratings.

I had heard through my friend and fellow wrestler Brad Kohler that the best match on the Midwest Indy's was Lenny Lane vs Scotty Z. It was guaranteed to be great in the ring, and the two guys had worked together over the years all the time and were real life friends. They would be willing to drive together from the Twin Cities. Brad was a guy who booked a few shows himself and was a jacked up powerhouse who also did MMA. Brad had a tremendous amateur wrestling background and seemed to be good friends with a lot of the Minnesota wrestlers who were top guys in the business. I respected his opinion, and he gave me Lenny's number.

Lenny had a nightly deal in WCW where he could still do Indy bookings. He kept busy and offered a reasonable rate. I asked him what he needed to come down and he said, "I don't know, three, three and a half?" Using my stellar negotiating tactics, I countered with $400 plus a hotel room! He immediately caved and agreed.

The show drew well with around three hundred fans! We pretty much broke even with the help of my friend Chad Ash selling sponsorships and Sarah and her sister selling concessions. James Grizzly wrestled a fantastic heel named Kamikaze Kid. They showed me what true heat was and how to structure a match so the heel gets maximum heat. When it was time for Griz to make his comeback, Kamikaze bumped and flew all over for him and the crowd ate it up.

Lenny showed up on time with Scotty following him a few

minutes later and shook everyone's hands. They were total pros and put on a fantastic match with a great finish. After the show was over, I met Lenny and Scotty at a bar downtown.

Scotty Zappa had been trying to get a contract with either of the big two companies for a year or so and had multiple dark matches and extra work under his belt. Scotty was in good shape at around 240 pounds and six foot tall or so. He belonged in the ring with Lenny and was a great guy to hang out with.

Lenny was really an interesting guy to talk to. Here was a guy pretty much my age who went to an average wrestling school and was from Wisconsin. Lenny was a little taller than me and worked hard in the gym, but he was no muscle man.

For the first time in my wrestling apprenticeship, I could see a guy who was just plain better than me at everything in wrestling. He could cut a better promo than me. He was far better than me in the ring, technically as well as how he interacted with the crowd. He carried himself like a star. Lenny was in better shape than me with a better "look." Lenny had better gear than me. There was absolutely nothing I could do better or even as well as him. He didn't have any advantages like being a second generation wrestler, better training, twenty years experience, or being a genetic monster. It was eye opening and humbling.

At the bar I flat out asked Lenny how he got as good as he was. Lenny said he took every booking he possibly could when he was starting. He said pay was the last thing on his mind; his focus was getting work. He told me a story about a promoter in Cleveland I think who paid terribly, but he ran a lot of shows. Lenny would not only take the poorly paid bookings, he would even tell the promoter he was willing to work two to three times on every show. Lenny would put on a mask and wrestle once. Then he'd come back for a singles match and then one more time for a tag.

Having read a self help book by Anthony Robbins, I understood the concept Lenny was telling me and the dividends it paid him. I would be lucky to wrestle once a month, maybe twice. I was getting prideful about my pay. People were telling me as a trained wrestler I should be getting $100 or at least $75.

95

So, at the end of a year I would have a dozen matches of experience. Lenny though would be getting booked every weekend, usually twice. If he worked three times every show, by the end of the year he had over three hundred matches! No wonder he was so much farther ahead than me. It was going to take me a decade to get his one year experience.

I simply was being outworked by Lenny.

When the bar closed, we headed to a greasy diner to eat. There Scotty and I buzzed up on beers, not having to work the next day, and ordered burgers and fries - lots of them. Despite having a few Bud Lights at the bar and it being late, Lenny ordered his breakfast - six egg whites with oatmeal and black coffee to drink. The lessons kept coming.

Lenny Lane: 2003

CHAPTER TWENTY-ONE

Hector Guerrero

Soon after my show with Lenny, I booked another card. This time the card was in nearby West Liberty, Iowa. West Liberty was a heavily populated Hispanic town of about 8,000 people with its biggest employer being a turkey processing factory.

At the time in WCW, Eddie Guerrero was involved in a strong story line with the Latino World Order. Eddie came from one of the greatest wrestling families in the world. His father Gory Guerrero was a great wrestler and a big star in Mexico teaming with the mythic El Santo before settling in El Paso, Texas. Gory was also a regional star in Texas helping draw Mexican American fans along with other Hispanics such as Jose Lothario and Ricky Romero.

Gory had four son who all became wrestlers, Eddie being the youngest. Chavo was a big star in Los Angeles, Texas, Japan, and Mid-South among other territories. Mando was a good wrestler who ended up being involved in the stunt business in Hollywood.

Hector Guerrero was a great wrestler I would try to get tapes of growing up, because his style was so unique. It was a combination of acrobatic high flying wrestling with a solid grounding in chain wrestling. Hector had a great head scissor out of the turnbuckle and a hybrid style that had been influenced by Lucha and his father's strong fundamental training. Hector also had a gymnastics background. While there was no doubt Eddie took his rich background and became the greatest of the brothers, I always enjoyed Hector and thought he was underrated.

I really enjoyed his short lived "Lazertron" masked gimmick he had in Jim Crockett's promotion in the Carolinas, even though I didn't know it was him. Unfortunately for Hector his one shot at the WWF was with the terrible "Gobbledy Gooker" gimmick that was an immediate and infamous failure.

Hector was past forty, but he had just finished up a run in WCW, where he wrestled his brother in a match on Monday Nitro that was a Guerreros fan's dream. Hector held his own and he and Eddie had a great short TV match. I was interested in booking him. I thought the Guerrero name would help draw, and Eddie being so strong on TV wouldn't hurt.

I picked Hector up at the airport late on a Friday night, and he was very talkative. I think he was just excited for the booking and happy to be on the road even if it was for just one shot.

Over the next two days, I got to spend a little time with him and learned a bit about the legendary family. Hector talked about his days in the Portland territory where one of the bookers would tell the guys to shoot wrestle in the first match or two. A shoot is a real wrestling match where both of you are trying to win the contest. The wrestlers would still do a worked match and then split the bonus for the shoot. The booker never seemed to know the difference!

He did confirm the family had a wrestling ring in their backyard, but it wasn't all fun as his dad would discipline them there if they misbehaved. He told me stories about my favorite promoter Bill Watts. Hector talked about working the Superdome in New Orleans and said the paydays were great. $1,000 paydays for just one night were common. That was damn good money for the early 80's in the business.

Hector had a good run in Mexico when it caught fire in the early 90's. Eddie was prominent in the promotion and helped Hector get booked. He talked about what it was like to go from being the young innovator with the cool new moves to being the older guy in the locker room surrounded by a new breed of Luchadores who were taking the sport to a new level. Psicosis, Rey Mysterio Jr, Eddie, and others were becoming some of the greatest wrestlers in all the world, better than the Japanese and top Americans. Hector had too much pride in his craft and family name. He said he spent time developing some new moves and worked hard to improve his work in the ring. I made note of that and really admired Hector for not settling into a routine and phoning it in.

Hector said he didn't mind the business being exposed as being fixed. "Do you like insulting people's intelligence?" he asked me. He said the business cost him his first marriage, but now he was a born again Christian and happily married. He had gotten his teaching certificate and was teaching in Alabama.

Hector had a good match against The Kamikaze Kid in West

Liberty, and we drew an okay crowd. Kamikaze was a willing bleeder and cut himself in order to get some blood and color for the Main Event. Also on the card were Griz, Travis Schillington, as well as two great wrestlers from Kansas and Missouri, Derek Stone and "The Atomic Dog" Steve Sharp. Brad Kohler brought his ring down for a bargain price and wrestled on the card as well, so we didn't lose too much money on the show.

Flying head scissors against Matty Star for IPW
Move stolen from Hector Guerrero. Photo: Miranda Cantrell

CHAPTER TWENTY-TWO

Learning The Ropes

As the summer came with not many bookings, I made it a point to ask for help. James Grizzly and I were talking on the phone and I asked Griz if he knew of any shows coming up. He mentioned there was a promoter in Kansas who was planning on running a lot of shows starting in late summer all the way through winter. He told me the pay wouldn't be the standard one hundred dollars or even the seventy-five dollars we independent wrestlers thought we deserved at that time, but it was work and maybe a lot of it. Griz gave me the number of the promoter, Dan Adams.

I called up Dan, and we talked for a bit. He asked how many matches I had and who trained me. He sounded like a decent guy, and he was clear they had intentions of running a lot of shows including some double shot weekends. Dan also told me the drives were going to be long as some of the shows were in Southern Kansas as well as parts of Missouri. It seemed the shortest drive would be Kansas City, over five hours away. When the topic of money came up, Dan made it clear there was no way I was going to get $100. He told me to send him a tape, if I was interested, and he would get back to me.

So, I sent a tape of my match with Travis in West liberty and placed an 8x10 picture with my resume on the back noting I spoke Spanish. A few weeks later Dan called me up and said my tape looked good and he was interested in booking me. I knew from talking to Griz and Derek Stone as well as my experience wrestling on a few shows in Missouri that the wrestlers there were not as well trained as other areas. This was because there weren't a lot of good training schools at that time in the area, and many of the veterans of the old Central States territory had long retired and weren't involved in the sport anymore. I got the feeling from Dan that despite my inexperience I was a decent guy to have on his cards and he was limited in booking quality young talent.

Dan seemed very sincere when he told me the absolutely best he could offer me was fifty dollars a show, with nothing for transportation and nothing for lodging. He was trying to book a lot of shows and taking a lot of risk. I also knew from running shows myself a promoter really couldn't pay everyone on the card as much as they would like. The economics just didn't allow it. I remembered my conversation with WCW wrestler Lenny Lane and told Dan I would take the bookings. Every single one. Dan said great. He gave me a date for the first show in late August and the city in Kansas.

The drive was long, the show was only twenty minutes from the Oklahoma border, and it didn't draw that well. But Dan was true to his word, he and his partner gave me my fifty dollars. Dan seemed to like me, my attitude, and my work. He told me if I was willing to come down I was booked on every show.

The next few months became my education in the world of independent wrestling. At some point in any wrestling career, you just have to work as much as possible. These shows gave me an education on traveling to different towns and wrestling in front of small crowds, some better and more receptive than others. I got to work with a variety of different wrestlers. Some were trained well, but if they were my age most were not. Sometimes despite my inexperience I was the best wrestler in the ring. I noticed a few guys spent time in the gym, but many did not. I began to appreciate my training with Alex Porteau and Skandar in Dallas more and more. I also realized, despite it only being two to three short years ago, the days of walking into the Sportatorium and seeing a locker room of veterans who worked the territories, knew TV, and drew money was gone.

One night I wrestled Griz in a rodeo barn with a dirt floor in front of about fifty people. But we had a good match and it was a rare good guy vs good guy match. I learned something in that match as Griz had to dig dip into his repertoire of moves so he didn't cheat. My respect for Griz's talent as a wrestler grew that night; I knew he carried me in the last three minutes of the match calling every single spot.

The next night Griz and I tagged up against a couple of veterans. It was a rare treat on the Indy scene. Our opponents were "Pretty Boy" Doug Masters and "Tiger" Treach Phillips Jr. I had heard of Treach as one day scouring the PWI match results I saw he worked Hector Guerrero at the Sportatorium for the

CWA when Grizzly Smith was involved.   My rookie mind figured Treach had to be good because if the CWA brought Hector in that cost them a little bit of money. When you invest some money on bringing a guy in, you can't just put him in with a piece of shit wrestler. Also, Hector worked a unique, fast-paced style, so you couldn't just put some plodding, heavyset wrestler in there with him either. As I shook hands with Treach, I figured he was in his mid thirties. I noticed he kept himself in great shape, and unlike most guys who were veterans he wasn't a giant - maybe around 210 pounds or so. He was a classic light heavyweight wrestler.

One more intangible was that Treach was a second generation wrestler. His father was a a Memphis wrestler who was a favorite of Elvis Presley. His dad even worked as a bodyguard for the King.

Second generation wrestlers just "get" our sport in a way mortals like me can't grasp. Hector Guerrero had explained it to me on the drive back to the airport. "Your parents told me you were a big fan of wrestling, always watching right?" I agreed and Hector continued, "Did you notice when you started in camp with Akbar that you picked up the moves quickly? Well, that was because you were always watching it, studying it without realizing it. When you're a second generation wrestler, it's like that but way way more because you grow up around it. It surrounds you." Sizing up Treach, I had a feeling I was going to learn something tonight.

Treach looked at me warily and made a point to say he'd wrestled with Griz before and knew he could work. He didn't say anything about me. Treach laid out a basic match with all four of us having a spot in the match. We went out and as the match started it was obvious Treach's partner, despite being overweight and not particularly athletic, knew what he was doing. I didn't know who Doug Masters was, but he was smooth and comfortable in the ring. I called a spot in the ring, and he got it right away and executed it perfectly.

Toward the end of the match, Treach and I were in the ring and he called a suplex. Now a suplex is a basic move, but honest

105

to God I'd never done one. I hesitated and Treach called me a dumb ass and took over the match. We finished the match, and Griz and I won.

In the back Treach was okay with me, but really didn't seem to want to talk to me. He had every reason to be unimpressed. I was still green and needed more experience. But my instincts about Treach were right as I saw him do high flying moves in there you didn't normally see most guys do, let alone a veteran. He worked a great style that I wanted to learn from. He easily could work Lucha as well as a Japanese style. I would compare him to a Brad Armstrong or Dean Malenko type with some good southern psychology.

I needed to get in the ring with him. I was willing to be called a dumb ass every night if it meant I was going to get better and learn. As I looked around the locker rooms of the Midwest, there just wasn't anyone like Treach in them. He was a veteran, second generation wrestler who could work a cruiser weight style and kept himself in shape. He could go in the ring. The shitty paydays and small crowds hadn't driven him away yet. He wasn't lazy in the ring or selfish either. I asked Dan Adams if I could have a match with him, and Dan said he'd do that for me on the next card.

CHAPTER TWENTY-THREE

Treach Phillips Jr.

The following weekend Treach and I worked the opening match. We had a few spots planned, but Treach as the heel and veteran was going to lead the match. As soon as we were introduced, Treach began getting his heat with the crowd, getting them fired up for the match and the night of wrestling that lay ahead. He was clearly defining who was the babyface and who was the heel in this match, always a hard thing for fans on the independent scene to grasp in the opener.

We circled for a bit and Treach did a couple front somersaults towards me that reminded me of the Guerrero's. He and I traded a few holds before I got the upper hand with a dropkick. Treach left the ring for a break on the floor and while he was outside regaining his composure he continued getting his heat with the crowd.

When we locked up again, he used an underhanded move to throw me outside the ring.   After landing outside, I sold for a brief time, far too brief considering I'd just landed on concrete. I saw Treach in the ring jawing with the crowd with his back turned to me. It seemed to me that the match had too little action going on, and I was getting restless. Treach was getting a reaction from the crowd, but I wasn't paying attention to that. All I cared about was that there were no moves happening. I slid back into the ring and nailed Treach in the back with a forearm. We went back to action in the ring. When I did that, I could hear the crowd's noise level drop.

Treach called me a dumb ass and asked me what the hell I was doing. I shut my mouth and listened to him the rest of the forgettable match. We went to a ten minute time limit draw. I could tell Treach was pissed, but I didn't know what I did wrong. I only knew we didn't have a good match and the crowd lost interest whenever I did something. But whenever Treach called something or worked the crowd, he got a response.

When we got to the back, Treach laid into me passionately. He began to implore me to not be in a hurry, to take my time. "Juan, when you ran into the ring after I threw you out, I was getting my heat. That's what I'm supposed to do, get heat!" After a couple minutes of him trying to not lose his temper while still helping me with this valuable feedback, exasperated Treach simply raised his voice and said, "Juan, it's not just about moves!"

In that moment a phrase I'd heard, but one I never truly understood, hit me. The light bulb went off. I got it. All the moves in the world didn't mean anything unless you did them at the right time in a match. Hell, most moves didn't mean as much as one good look, a smirk from a heel, or a look of determination from the babyface hero, some fire. If I didn't sell those moves, why were we doing them? Treach was also getting heat from the crowd, all I should have been doing was selling and gaining sympathy. Instead, I was rushing to the next move.

Treach tried to finish up by being encouraging. He told me I was good, and I could improve. He told me to pay attention, and he'd be happy to work with me again. "Juan, we can get you to the point we'll have the crowd dying to see one of those moves off the top rope from you." But he made it clear that you worked to that point to get the most reaction out of it.

I changed and watched the rest of the card. That night Little Kato and Beautiful Bobby, two legendary midget wrestlers out of St. Joseph, Missouri put on a clinic. They were fantastic and so entertaining.

The rest of the week I just kept thinking about that match and what went wrong as well as Treach's words. I let those words and lessons settle in my head. It was really a turning point for me in what pro wrestling was all about. I always was thinking about my moves and high spots. I wasn't thinking about how to interact with the crowd even at a basic level. I slowly was learning bits and pieces about the craft. It only reinforced in my head the fact I had to work with people better than me and veterans. I also was learning I wasn't as good as I thought. It seemed I had so much to learn. But I was encouraged that at least I was becoming aware of this, and now I could try to improve my work in the ring.

Dan Adams and his partner were also taking care of me. They always paid me my $50 regardless of the crowd. Dan's partner came up to me many nights and would ask me if I had a hotel in the city. I would tell him I didn't. He would pull out a hotel key card and hand it to me to the local Ramada or Super 8. He cleaned pools for many of these hotels and was getting a few comps. He would give me my very own room. One time he paid a room out of his own pocket and told me I could stay there for free. He told me he appreciated the fact I drove from so far away, he liked my attitude, and he thought I wrestled pretty well. I think he liked that I showed up on time, never was worried about getting stoned or drunk, and was just grateful for the experience. I wish I remembered his name as I never got to thank him for his generosity.

I was loving working so often, every weekend sometimes Saturday and Sundays. I was meeting some nice, talented people who all were helpful and generous with their time for me. One weekend we wrestled in Kansas City, and I shook hands with an older black gentleman named Tom Jones. Tom told me he lived in Oklahoma. As soon as he said that, I immediately asked him if he had ever worked for Bill Watts and he said he had. I asked him what he thought of Watts, and he said he liked him. I asked why, and he simply said, "He ran things the way they're supposed to be."

Tom talked to me about Skandar Akbar and and Mid South wrestling for a few hours. Dan and his partner were having a show in a high end country music bar and treated the wrestlers to some catered Kansas City BBQ. Tom and I sat down while I asked questions and he talked over some delicious free brisket and pulled pork with all the fixings. Tom was so soft spoken and kind that it was amazing he'd survived so many years in the tough business of wrestling. He reminded me a lot of Skandar.

I never knew how long of a career "Mr. Ebony" Tom Jones had until many years after that wonderful conversation. Tom had held titles all over the country, but he was especially successful in the South. He made a bit of history in Mid South when Watts was determined to have a first ever match in Mississippi between a black man vs a white man. Watts wanted to have the good guy be the black athlete and the white wrestler the bad guy or heel. It was a risky thing to do in the South in the early 70's. Who did Watts pick to be in this historical color barrier breaking match?

110

He picked Tom Jones.

That night an old Central States tag team the Batten twins worked the Main Event. They were so fast paced and had great teamwork. They reminded me of many of those great southern tag teams. In the locker room while I was lacing up my boots, I saw all the names of the acts who had worked at this bar before they hit the big time. The Dixie Chicks had signed their names on the wall along with, "You guys have got big dicks in Kansas City!"

The following weekend we wrestled near the hometown of "Hangman" Bobby Jaggers.   The ring announcer did a fantastic job introducing him to the crowd as a retired wrestler, and Bobby appreciated the great introduction. I talked with him for twenty minutes or so, and he treated me as a contemporary. He introduced me to his teenage kids, and we talked about his times in Puerto Rico and a bit about Southwest Championship out of San Antonio.

Texas Journeyman Dusty Wolf was on that double shot wearing a fanny pack. He wrestled Tom Jones in a match and, though he did a lot of stalling, it was good. I also wasn't even thinking I was as good as Dusty was now that I was appreciating these veterans. I was proud of the fact that at that time people said you weren't part of the business unless you knew Dusty or were on a card with him.

In the main event that night was Tommy Rogers, one half of the tag team The Fantastics. Tommy looked in incredible shape, ready for another run in a top promotion. Soon he was on E.C.W. television.

Weekend after weekend I was getting better by simply getting work. Every match was an opportunity to try something new or different in the ring and get that instant feedback. Dan would share with me his insights on why he booked the matches a certain way. He would explain why one guy lost and the other one won. He would talk to me on the phone occasionally and just kept booking me. Yet, it was becoming apparent that Dan and his partner were losing money on most of these shows and it wasn't going to go on forever. Finally, the inevitable happened and the two partners split up with the shows stopping in the winter.

I was very grateful to Dan and his partner for the chance to get so much work. It was a huge step in me gaining experience and feeling more comfortable in the ring. They always treated me well and were true to their words. To this day I think about those shows that fall and winter as being my education of a wrestler.

Now I knew what I wanted to try next. My buddy James Grizzly had told me the legendary former NWA world champion Harley Race was opening up his own promotion in Missouri. Griz had already been booked by Harley a few times and was becoming a mainstay in his promotion. I did what Ron and I had done a year before. I bought a ticket to Harley's WLW show he was promoting and brought my resume and tape. Grizzly told me he would introduce me to Harley after the show. I watched a great card with The One Man Gang, Griz, Derek Stone, Mr. Destiny Jay Hannah, and a very green and young Trevor Murdoch.

Sure enough, after the show when he finished wrestling Griz introduced me to Harley. On the resume I noted that I spoke Spanish along with my training and experience. Harley was polite, but only said he would consider me. I drove the five hours home wondering if the mileage and money spent would be worth it, but I understood there was nothing that was going to replace meeting Harley in person.

A few weeks later, I came home to my trailer after work and on my answering machine was the gravely voice of Harley Race. "Juan, I'd like to have you come down to California, Missouri and a few other shows. Give me a call if you're interested."

CHAPTER TWENTY-FOUR

Harley Race

Harley Race is a living legend. Ric Flair has said many times the toughest guy he'd ever been in the ring with was Harley. A seven time NWA world heavyweight champion he was, in my opinion, the greatest wrestler in the world in the late 70's after Jack Briscoe and the Funk brothers began slowing down just a step. He remained the man until a young, bleached-blond, brash wrestler from Minneapolis began to make a name for himself in the Carolina territories. For five years or so, he was the best. I'd never met anyone ever who was the best in the world at what they did. It's pretty humbling when you think about it, that kind of excellence.

Harley was just finishing up his last run as world champion when I became a fan in the early 80's. I remembered seeing Ric Flair on the cover of Pro Wrestling Illustrated with a bandage on his forehead with the magazine title, "A Second Chance at Greatness" after he beat Harley for the strap in the very first Starcade.

Harley worked some territories afterward then retired from the ring to become a successful manager in WCW. After a car accident, he was let go and went through some tough financial and personal struggles. He got back into the only business he really ever knew again with the help of his wife B.J. and started W.L.W., an independent promotion as well as a training school.

Harley was planning a series of cards in the Midwest and booked me for a show in Des Moines and two other cards. He told me on the phone he wanted to book me in California, Missouri, as they had a large Hispanic population he wanted to try to market to. He asked me if I would be able to do some radio interviews in Spanish and I told him I could. I actually had a little bit of doubt about the radio interviews. My Spanish was just okay and the thought of talking to a host over the phone in only Spanish without the benefit of eye contact and English as a backup was not something I was sure I could do. I expressed my doubts over the phone with my fellow wrestler Travis Schillington. Travis said I shouldn't worry about it. He said, "Juan, I can't speak Spanish and neither can Harley. How the hell is he going to know if your Spanish is good or if it sucks?"

I was still apprehensive, so I talked to my brother Jorge and my Dad about the interviews. I wanted to learn the proper words in Spanish for fans, support, and ring. The kind of words that I would have to use to express myself when talking about wrestling, not ordering dinner at the local Mexican restaurant. I spent about an hour going over and practicing my interview with them. I felt much more confident and ready after the prep work. I called in to the Spanish station and the host was fantastic. He walked me through the interview and it went off without a hitch.

The first show in the run was in Des Moines, and I wrestled Griz in the opener and the match went well. I had the next night off as Harley was running a show in Kansas City. The following night was my show in California, Missouri.

Harley told me leading up to the show that he was going to have some WCW wrestlers there from the main roster as well as some guys from the Power Plant. Harley had tremendous connections to both companies and was able to land a few veterans who weren't being used regularly such as The Barbarian and Beautiful Bobby Eaton. The new wrestlers from the Power Plant would get a great opportunity to get some experience in front of a more forgiving crowd on these smaller shows. Their mistakes wouldn't be exposed in the glare of a highly-rated, national TV show. Harley got great talent to put on his card with some star power, we got a chance to work with some great veterans and up-and-coming talent. It was a win-win for all involved.

Harley informed me a couple weeks before the show that I would be in a tag match with a Power Plant guy named Chuck Palumbo. We would be tagging against Griz and The Barbarian. It would be my first time wrestling with a name, a guy who I'd seen on TV for years who had competed in Wrestlemania and numerous pay-per-views. I was excited and nervous.

As soon as I got to the show, Harley told me we would be driving to the radio station for some interviews in Spanish again. I got into the car with Harley and as we talked he gave me a few tidbits I could share on the radio. Harley had wrestled the two biggest names in Mexican wrestling history, Mil Mascaras and El

Santo.

Mascaras I was aware of from pictures I'd seen of the 70's with Harley and him battling for the world title. Mascaras was a huge global star and drawing card in the 70's. His fame in Japan had inspired many young Japanese wrestlers with his colorful masks, capes, and tights. He had a very superhero look, a great physique, and his lucha libre skills were a style Japan hadn't seen a lot of. He created a sensation there and toured Japan extensively.

In the States, Mascaras was the very first masked wrestler to perform in Madison Square Garden as masked wrestlers were banned prior to him. His ability to speak English combined with his unusual size for a Mexican (He was a former, competitive bodybuilder and he stood around six foot and weighed a muscular 240 pounds.) opened doors for him which other talented Mexicans couldn't get through. Hispanic fans are some of the most loyal fanatics of wrestling and the burgeoning immigrant populations in Houston, Dallas, Los Angeles, and all over the states made Mascaras in great demand as a headliner and specialty attraction.

If that wasn't enough, Mascaras had starred in numerous lucha libre movies that developed a cult following all over the world. A former amateur wrestler who had a legitimate shot at making the Mexican Olympic team, he carried himself as a star from his very first match. His background in amateur wrestling as well as Judo kept him from being pushed around in the ring.

The magazines loved him, because he was so very colorful and different. Years later I met Bil Apter and George Napolitano, two photographers who did the vast majority of the picture taking for the major magazines. They told me they loved Mascaras. Color pictures were still new, and most wrestlers still wore dull, bland gear. Mascaras had a tan, chiseled physique, and his colorful gear he constantly updated and changed fit the times perfectly. He was exotic and international, and they put him on their covers numerous times.

The other Mexican legend Harley had worked was El Santo. My dad had always talked of reading comic books of Santo and he is an iconic figure in Mexican history - not Mexican wrestling history, but **Mexican** History. He was the trailblazer of the masked lucha movies during their golden age. When he died, he was buried in his mask, and it made national news all over the country. It could be argued that no other wrestler in any country was more popular and loved than him. He kept his identity an obsessive secret only revealing a glimpse of his face on national TV once months before his death.

Harley told me on the drive over to the station he was scheduled to work Santo in the border town of El Paso. He drove to the show with Terry Funk and Funk gave him the information on Santo. How popular he was with Mexican fans, but also how short he was and his small stature. Harley told me he was having his doubts about putting over this guy who wore a hood and was so small he'd never heard of. As he and Funk pulled up to the arena, Harley saw the line of fans spilling around the block, almost all of them Mexican fans there to see their hero. Harley turned to Funk and said, "Whatever he wants to do!"

The interview went great, and Harley asked the host how my Spanish was. The host said it was very good. I was relieved that I could come through for Harley. Now it was time to head back to the show and figure out my tag match.

Griz was there to meet me and immediately tried to rib me. He told me he's been telling Barbarian I was going around saying he had a small Samoan dick. He told me Barbarian was getting hot and was going to pay me back in the ring. I figured Griz was full of it, but I still made it a point to go up the Barbarian, shake his hand, and introduce myself as soon as I saw him. He didn't know who I was was, and it confirmed my feeling Griz was just messing with me.

I met Chuck Palumbo soon after. We all four got together and started to lay out our match. We did the natural thing and shut up while Barbarian came up with the blueprint of our bout. Barbarian was open to ideas and asked us during key points what we could do and used our strengths to make the match better. After I got cut off and they started their heat, he had an idea for me taking a backdrop from Griz and he would catch me and turn it into a power bomb. It was a potentially dangerous move, but I trusted Griz and Barbarian both had the strength to protect me the whole time. Barbarian wanted to make sure I felt comfortable with the spot. He let me and Griz come up with our final finish at the end of the match while he and Palumbo would fight outside. When we were all confident with having a basic match laid out where we would call most of the heat in the ring, we went to get changed.

Palumbo and I went to our section of the locker room. As Palumbo took his shirt off, I saw a guy who had a tremendous look for the business. He was tall, over six foot four I thought. Chuck was tan and had a great build. He seemed athletic, had a rock star haircut, and wore leopard trunks. He looked like a real life Tarzan. As ridiculous as it sounded, I was going to be the whitest guy in the ring with these three. As I saw my plain black biker short tights, my untanned skin, and average build I knew I had more work to do.

Palumbo was a pretty good guy, and I suggested we slap hands as we walked to the ring. Harley had a young, Hispanic student form the local school introduce the match in Spanish as well as English. The crowd was a good one with around five hundred enthusiastic fans who were excited to be there.

I started off the match with Griz, and I got some good offense on him that got the crowd behind me. I was worried I wouldn't look like I belonged in the ring with these three. The beginning of the match helped me show I deserved to be there. When Barbarian tagged in, the crowd noticeably responded. It was a mix of excitement, concern for me, and anticipation of this big, bad, Samoan dude causing some havoc.

I sold through my body language Barbarian's size and presence. We stared off for a few brief seconds when I slowly turned to my partner Palumbo who was eager to tag in and face off with the big man. The crowd picked up on it and began to clamor for the tag. So simple, but so effective I thought. I asked the crowd if they wanted Palumbo tagged in, and when they cheered I tagged.

Palumbo and Barbarian faced off and this match up seemed a

118

lot more equal. The crowd watched the stare down with anticipation. When Chuck hit Barbarian with a couple tackles to no avail, he then leapfrogged him and hit him with a big dropkick that sent Barbarian out of the ring. The crowd erupted! Griz rushed into the ring only to suffer the same fate at the hands of Palumbo's dropkick. As I went into the ring to high five Palumbo, Griz and Barbarian huddled together outside the ring. I inched to the ropes and leaped from inside the ring outside hitting a Mexican plancha or flying body press onto our two opponents and knocking them both down. The crowd was now firmly behind both Palumbo and me.

As the crowd settled down, Palumbo worked over Griz and we tagged in back and forth working over Griz's arm before it was time for us to do our big power spot to start the heat. Griz finally got the tag to Barbarian while I was in the ring. I hit Barbarian with a couple dropkicks and staggered him. When I went for the Lou Thesz press, Barbarian caught me in midair. The crowd knew I was in trouble and groaned. As Barbarian held me in a bear hug, Griz hit the ropes and nailed me with a Hart Foundation type clothesline.

As they pounded me, I tried to rally the crowd. It was time for the big power spot and Griz tagged in Barbarian, he threw me to the ropes and backdropped me. As I flipped over Griz, I could tell I was landing a bit short as Barbarian grabbed me. Using his incredible raw power, he caught me as I was going down. He stopped me from dropping, lifting my 225 pounds up with ease into a power bomb position. As he held me, the crowd knew what was coming for their young, undersized good guy and Barbarian planted me flat on my back in the middle of the ring. The crowd murmured with a combination of sympathy for me and astonishment at this Samoan's power. Barbarian's incredible strength took care of me the entire time and actually saved me from landing on my head when I got back flipped. To this day I'm convinced if an average wrestler had been the one to catch me from that backdrop I'd have been injured.

The crowd stayed with us the entire match imploring Chuck Palumbo to make the tag and clean house. When he did, the crowd cheered and we went to our finish in the match. Harley had asked me my finishing move earlier in the evening and I said Frankensteiner off the top rope. Harley said to use that as I was getting the pin. So, Griz and I set up the move and when I hit the Frankensteiner, a leg scissors executed on my opponent while he sits on the top rope, the crowd popped when the referee Skippy counted to three.

It was a great match, and we were all very happy with it. Harley's son-in-law said it was the best match of the night, and I agreed. It felt good to deliver in a match in front of the legendary Harley Race wrestling for the first time with a star like The Barbarian. There's a great You Tube video of him working out with Mr Olympia Lee Haney if you want to check out Barbarian's size and power. Barbarian was so very gracious to us before the match and in the match he was light, never stiff despite his incredible reputation as a real-life, tough guy. I remembered Barbarian wrestling the great Tito Santana in Wrestlemania 6 and here I got to wrestle with him. It was a great experience.

It also felt good that I was able to execute my part of the match. Palumbo wasn't any better of a mechanical wrestler than I was. He also made a minor mistake in the match and showed me we weren't miles apart in wrestling ability. But there was no doubt, he was way ahead of me on his look and his appeal as a star. Some of it I couldn't do anything about like my height or genetics for putting on that kind of size. Yet, there was no doubt I could improve that part of my character, my look much more.

Just a few months later, I began to see Chuck Palumbo on WCW Television. Eventually, he had a good run for WWE as well. From what I could tell in my one match with him, he deserved his time in the big time.

CHAPTER TWENTY-FIVE

Blue Collar Job

After working for Harley Race, I felt his promotion was the place to be in the Midwest. Finally, there was someone in the Heartland who was a legitimate, experienced veteran running a school and a promotion. Harley had contacts to both WCW and WWE as well as Japan.

However, I had some challenges and forks in the road to deal with before I could decide my next focus in wrestling. First, I had applied for a full-time job at my local factory job at a chemical plant. I had been working as a temp at the plant after my temp gig at Bandag ended. The plant was one of the best factory jobs in town. It paid extremely well, had great benefits including a pension, 401k, insurance, and four weeks vacation. When I walked into the room of the local Holiday Inn to apply, I knew there were over nine hundred people applying for about twenty jobs. I was one of one hundred who landed an interview.

When I was interviewing for the job, one of the questions I was asked by one of the long-time employees at the plant was, "I noticed on your resume that you've held several different jobs at several different employers.   Can you explain that?"

I told him I had always left those other jobs for wrestling, and that at the age of twenty-six I didn't feel I was ever going to wrestle for the WWE. Getting a job at the WWE was like trying to be a rock star or a Nascar driver, and it just wasn't happening. Later in the interview, I was asked by a different set of people about my dream job. I answered honestly that I wouldn't like anything more than to be a full-time wrestler traveling the world and getting paid well to do it.

A couple weeks later Jeff, a full-time employee, handed me the phone while I was on break. He said, "It's Jenny from H.R." With other employees and temps who also applied for those twenty great jobs looking on, I picked up the phone. Jenny offered me a full-time job - one that thousands of people in town would love to have offered to them. I accepted the job without hesitation.

I knew that for the very first time in my life if I ever wanted to pursue something in wrestling that demanded me to move or extensive travel I had something to lose. This was was not a job at Hardees. It was a full-time job that people spent their lives at. They raised families, took nice vacations, paid for college, and bought homes with this job. If you played your cards right by investing in the company 401K, living reasonably, and investing your money well, you could walk out of the plant set for life. By carrying a lunch bucket to work and working swing shift with a high school diploma, you could retire comfortably.

I knew I was at a crossroads, and I had made a decision that would limit my dreams in wrestling. However, I didn't feel I had the luxury to turn down this opportunity. At this point in my career, I hadn't really seen anyone on my level rise above the Indy's and make it. I also didn't see why I couldn't keep doing what I was doing already - working the regular job and wrestling on the weekends. I had a hunch but no guarantee I was going to be sent back to my area I worked as a temp where we had weekends off. I would make far more money than I was currently making and would have more security.

But it wasn't long after I took the full-time job that I got married then divorced soon after from Sarah. It was all my fault as I wasn't mature enough and ready for a relationship. Despite the fact the marriage imploded from my own mistakes and lack of maturity, it was painful. I had disappointed my family and had hurt a sweet girl who never did anything but support and care about me. For the first time in my life, my selfishness and lack of maturity had caused real pain in many people's lives. Pain I caused through my own bad decisions and actions.

CHAPTER TWENTY-SIX

Back To Camp

Now I had all the time in the world and money to pursue my dream, I thought. Even if I didn't feel I could make it to the WWE, I thought I could try to get a dark match or tryout match as they called them in those days. I moved back in with my parents temporarily and began to hit the gym and adjust to this single life after years of being in a relationship.

It was harder than I thought it would be. I was lonely after being used to the companionship of a relationship. I began to partake in the bar scene, something I had never really done before. Going to the bar after work and on the weekends became a regular occurrence.

Despite the fact the bar scene became my constant companion, I continued to train hard. My friend Jim Dipple became my training partner, and we began to tear it up in the weight room at the Y. Jim was a perfect guy to train with at the time, because he was bigger and stronger than me. He pushed me and kept me consistent. He wasn't judgmental of my personal problems that I was going through at the time, and we hung out a lot during our free time as well.

Even though I was drinking a lot and not paying attention to my diet, I had just turned twenty-seven and was training hard. Because I was in my prime physically, I was looking fit. I thought about what would be the best thing for me to do with my wrestling, since the phone wasn't ringing with many booking offers.

I decided to train at Harley's school in Eldon, Missouri. It was a five-hour drive, but according to Harley I could train during the weekends and pay the reduced rate of $1,000 since I was already experienced. I figured I could use the ring time and additional training. I believed Harley would start booking me more often if I was one of his students. I had the time and money, and I was in great shape.

I went down to Harley's school Labor Day weekend 2000. The day I went down they were having an open tryout. Trevor Murdoch, Matt Murphy, and my old friend James Grizzly were at the tryout helping out and were all living in Eldon to stay close to where the action was. I worked out along with the people trying

125

out. I went through the calisthenics and Hindu Squats that the ex-Marine referee Skippy put people through.

As a few began to drop out, I continued. This time I was prepared for the workout. It was still tough and demanding, but I had spent the past couple months doing the calisthenics two to three times a week to get ready. Still halfway through the tryout, I was happy to hear Skippy tell the new people, myself, and another experienced wrestler didn't have to continue the exercises. We sat down and took a break.

I was surprised to find out the trainer at the time was Skippy. No offense to Skippy, but I didn't feel I was going to learn as much from him as I would have from Derek Stone, the previous trainer, or someone like Griz. I tried to keep a positive attitude and knew I still could learn and improve from being around Harley and the WLW crew.

That first night I spent at the nearby hotel told me this was going to be harder than I thought. Though I had once driven seven hours straight to Dallas from Eagle Pass when I was training with Skandar Akbar, the five-hour drive to Eldon had seemed long. I also was still dealing with the divorce. I wasn't very good about being alone, something I had never struggled with previously. I was questioning whether I really wanted to be there, basically starting over.

I did learn some tremendous conditioning exercises from Skip. He was the first guy to teach me about working a body part when I was working out with Tim Vein, a good Native American wrestler who was improving under Harley's training. One weekend, Derek Stone showed up, and we got to work an impromptu tag match in front of a small crowd of kids as downtown Eldon was having a celebration.

I got booked by Harley in the fall for a show that featured Butch Reed on the card. A former regional and national star, Butch still looked great with big arms. I made it a point to sit next to him after we all had settled in to change. I introduced myself, and when he asked I told him I'd been trained by Ak. Reed instantly changed his demeanor, becoming almost wistful. He told me Ak had been booking the Mid-South territory when he started there. "Skandar made me the brass knuckles champ. He helped me a lot. Love Ak, great guy."

Reed had been a favorite of Bill Watts for years and worked steadily in Mid-South leaving only occasionally when he was becoming overexposed. A black athlete and a tough guy who had good size, he was the kind of wrestler Watts loved. He headlined the territory as a heel and a babyface who was just a step below the territories most over wrestler in history, The Junkyard Dog.

Reed went to the WWF after the territories began to dry up. He was on the famous Wrestlemania 3 card that was headlined by Hogan vs Andre The Giant in front of the largest wrestling crowd in history at the time - 93,000. After his time in WWF, he worked for WCW as one half of the outstanding tag team of Doom with the college football star Ron Simmons. They held the world tag belts and were having tremendous hard-hitting matches with teams like the Steiner Brothers. Now, Reed was paying the business back helping Harley out on this independent shows. He would be wrestling my buddy Griz in the main event.

As I talked with Reed about my favorite promotion of Mid-South, I asked him a question I was beginning to wonder about this wonderful craft of professional wrestling. "How long did it take you to know what you were doing in the ring, really feel like you belonged in there?"

His answer humbled me. He thought long and hard about it and was silent for about 20 seconds before he responded, "Probably five years, man."

To clarify I asked, "Five years of full-time, five years of working the territories?"

"Yeah, man, five years of six days a week. Five years of being in there with people better than me."

Next, he talked to me about working Harley when he was still in his first year or two. "Man, we went an hour. I was blown up so bad, and all he did was keep coming up with more spots! I'd never heard of so many damn spots!"

Must have been a hell of an experience to have been in the ring with Harley in the 70's when he was NWA World Heavyweight Champion. Back in those days the guys dressed in separate locker rooms, and you never talked with your opponent before the match.   Then to have to go an hour with the champ. When the champ left town the next night, you were left in the territory having to still look strong, have people believe in you, and be able to draw. You would grow so much as a performer.

I got dressed and had a good match with Tim Vein in a good guy vs good guy bout. I heard some faint boos and fans heckling me in the match about my nationality. None of it was too bad. No racial slurs, but things like, "Go home to Mexico! Where's your tacos?" The same thing had happened twice before in other matches. I thought maybe I could turn some of that little bit of heat into something if I tried. It seemed the smaller the town if I didn't wrestle as a babyface against a clear-cut, strong heel, if there was any ambiguity, they reacted toward me as the default heel. It got me wondering what would happen if I really poured on the gasoline. What if I really gave them someone to hate?

I finished dressing and looked on as Butch Reed went over his match with my buddy Griz. They had a solid match, and Griz got the victory over the veteran Reed making him look so strong. I was impressed with Reed, he was a class act. Still in shape, he was giving back to the biz and Harley who had taken care of him so many years ago when Reed was a rookie. He was helping make Griz and helping draw a bit with his name on the card. I was learning slowly about this wonderful business and its traditions. No one was bigger than the business. We all had an obligation to give back to it after drinking from its well.

CHAPTER TWENTY-SEVEN

Fly On The Wall

My idea of training with Harley on the weekends wasn't getting anywhere. Skippy was still the trainer, and I was losing my motivation to drive five hours one way for these sessions. Harley rarely watched or participated. I think he was very active during the week, but on weekends he was busy with other things and enjoying some much needed time for rest and relaxation. Skippy knew as much about wrestling as I did and was a great ref also. Yet, I felt I needed to work and train with someone who was much better and far more experienced than I was in order to improve.

The biggest problem was me though. I was training hard in the gym after working all week at the plant, but I was more interested in spending my weekends at the bar or trying to meet girls. I began to miss some of my weekend training sessions, choosing instead to work overtime at the plant or just stay in town.

I was willing to give up my weekends for a booking, but Harley wasn't booking me and neither was anyone else. I couldn't blame Harley or other promoters for not considering me. I wasn't getting in front of people. The phone wasn't ringing, and I wasn't out hustling trying to make contacts and my own breaks. The end of my going to Eldon was one Saturday or Sunday morning that winter when my phone rang. I was in bed with a girl when I answered. Skippy asked me if I was coming down for training, and I made up a bullshit excuse that I was working overtime. I think we both knew I was not coming back.

Fortunately, Harley needed some bodies for a WWF Monday Night Raw in St Louis in February of 2001. Harley had a lot of pull and when the WWF needed some talent for a few matches Harley was able to book Griz, Superstar Steve, Matt Murphy, Derek Stone, and The Drill Instructor for some enhancement matches.

Harley was asked to supply some independent wrestlers for a TV skit also as extras. Harley called and asked me if I was interested and able to be there Monday. Of course, I said yes.

Pulling up to the arena in downtown St. Louis, I saw Harley at an entrance to the backstage area. He led me to where I needed to be, and I sat down with some of my fellow Indy wrestlers such as Jay Hanna and Travis. Referee Dave Hepner and agent Tony Garea took down our information for payroll purposes and then proceeded to hand us $250 cash for our work that day! I would have done it for free of course.

The agents told us they would need us to be extras on a segment involving The Acolytes. The Acolytes were made up of legendary college football star Ron Simmons who was a former WCW Heavyweight Champion and the big Texan I worked out with in Dallas at Doug's Gym Bradshaw, the former John Hawk.

The segment was going to be filmed at a strip bar on the Illinois side of St. Louis. What a rough gig, I thought. Paid more than I ever had for a show, no painful bumps, and I got to be a fly on a wall on a national TV show all while looking at naked, young women.

While we waited for our directions to the strip club, we all sat trying to be cool while The Undertaker walked in and shook hands with Triple H. Then the leader of the company Stone Cold Steve Austin walked by with a cup of coffee. All around us were the stars of the WWF during the hottest time in the history of the company. People were all running around preparing for the most important two hours of live television they did every week.

We left to find the strip club and carpooled together. At the club, we saw Bruce Pritchard, one of Vince McMahon's lieutenants, and television producers directing the segment. Just as they told us, they simply wanted us to be audience members. They figured as Indy wrestlers we would not bother the wrestlers by asking them for autographs or generally interrupting the shoot. We knew why we were there, and all of us behaved professionally. We stayed out of the way and, if we had to get involved physically in the shoot during the altercation part, we would know how to take a shot.

The shoot was all done in one take with it ending in violence when the opposing team of Val Venis and his teammates ambushed the Acolytes. My buddy T.S. had to take a punch and got laid out. It was all good for Trav though as he appeared on TV knocked out.

131

After the shoot, I saw Bradshaw in the bathroom cleaning up the cut he got over his eye. He was tending to his cut and still pumped from the segment, so I wasn't surprised that he didn't recognize me. Plus, it had been several years since we had seen each other.

We all headed back to the arena and were told we were welcome to eat at catering. We enjoyed lunch with Dwayne Johnson, The Rock, sitting near us while he talked to Terri Runnels. I wished Griz luck in his match against Perry Saturn, and we headed to the seats we were given as comps to watch the show.

I booked a show with my friend Derek Bates in March trying to make something happen. It was on March 10th, 2001, the day before my birthday. I booked several of the WLW crew such as Griz, Matt Murphy, Derek Stone, Superstar Steve, as well as Skippy to ref. From Minnesota, we brought in Lenny Lane with Scotty Zappa and Chi Town Thug. Travis Schillington brought the ring and Mr. Destiny Jay Hanna worked the main event against Lenny.

It was a good show that drew okay. In the locker room, Lenny asked if he could come up with his own finish. I said that was fine as I trusted Lenny to keep things reasonably family friendly and he was way more creative and experienced with finishes than I was. Lenny also asked if he could add a little humor and edge. "Hey, Juan, sometimes I come out to the ring with a sock stuffed into my trunks. Then when I get announced I just stand there and pose. It's not as obvious with these trunks, but it still gets a good reaction! You can see the women in the audience looking at each other like, 'Do you see that?'"

I laughed and told Lenny that would be fine. I heard the crowd pop in the locker room before Skippy counted to three, so I figured the finish was good.

At the bar afterward, I saw my friend from work Stretch who went to the show with his son Anthony. He said he loved the way the main event ended. I heard several people say it was great, so I went to Skippy and asked about the finish.

Skippy took a drag of his cigarette and said with a smile, "Well, it wasn't a Harley finish. After Lenny wrestled the whole match with his sock in his trunks, Jay and him did a spot where the sock fell out. Lenny picked up the sock and sold it to the crowd that he wasn't really that endowed. Then Jay hit his finisher!" I thought it was a great entertaining, edgy finish without offending the parents in the audience as the joke would go over most kids' heads.

I met an Iowa promoter at the bar who was getting ready to have one of his first shows named Troy Peterson. He was very nice and complimentary on the show. Even though I knew he had a show coming up in Oskaloosa, Iowa, only a couple of hours away and he was standing right in front of me, I didn't ask if he would be interested in booking me. I knew he was booking Travis, Griz, and numerous Midwest talents. I figured he knew who I was and didn't book me because he wasn't interested in booking me.

As the clock struck midnight, I turned twenty-eight. I was not progressing in wrestling, and I began to feel the hands of time slowly beginning to work against me. I knew if I didn't make something happen before I was thirty, I was probably going to be out of time. I had a great job, and I was getting ready to close on my first house. Things were going well in life, just not in wrestling.

CHAPTER TWENTY-EIGHT

Opportunity Lost

I spent the rest of the spring not even pursuing wrestling. I still trained in the gym, but for all intents and purposes I wasn't doing anything. I got a phone call in the summer of 2001 from Harley offering a great opportunity.

All Japan was one of the two biggest promotions in Japan and its legendary founder Giant Baba had recently passed away. Baba had left the company to his widow and the male dominated business and wrestling culture in Japan was struggling with the concept of a female owner. Several of its top stars made a bold exit and formed their own company, NOAH.

One of its owners, bookers, and the top star of the promotion was Misawa. He was making a trip to the U.S. and other countries looking for talent to fill out their roster. Harley had a long standing relationship with the old company of All Japan and was revered in the country when he was the traveling NWA World Heavyweight Champion.

NOAH and Harley had set up a tryout in Eldon for independent wrestlers. Harley invited all his students and talent he knew to the tryout. When he called me, Harley gave me the date and let me know Misawa was looking to book talent for two upcoming tours.

Japan was considered a part of a wrestlers development in their career. They had a hard-hitting, physical style of wrestling. Everything from the in ring work to the promotion and dealing with the press was done in such a manner to make the sport as legitimate as possible.

It was a place some wrestlers made a full-time career at such as Stan Hansen. Hansen made a fortune in Japan and only occasionally worked Stateside. When he did work for a prominent promotion such as the AWA, he always put his Japan dates and reputation there on the forefront.

Other wrestlers made it their primary focus such as Bruiser Brody and the Funk brothers at times in their career. They were making the majority of their living there and only working as much or as little as they wanted in the U.S.

Almost all the top stars in the U.S. though did tours of Japan in their careers. The several week long tours were lucrative and

135

most guys earned far more than they did in the territories.

If I heard or read about a top star who didn't work in Japan a lot, it usually was due to a few factors. Some simply didn't like the food and culture and went crazy there for the tours. A few big names such as Jerry Lawler and Ric Flair before he became N.W.A. champion made just as much or even more money in their strong territories on top without the long plane flights and tough tours. Lawler didn't have a wrestling style that fit Japan either and wasn't crazy about the all the details that came with the tours.

For smaller wrestlers, it was a godsend. Until the mid 90's, a wrestler under six foot and weighing less than 230 pounds knew he was limited in how far he could rise in wrestling. Eddie Guerrero wrote in his book he always felt Japan was where he needed to be to make a good living and made it his ultimate goal until the business slowly began to change in the States. My trainer Alex Porteau did a few tours and made far more money there than he ever did anywhere else at the time.

I was aware of all this as I thought about the opportunity Harley was handing me. Nowadays, many young guys have to pay for the rare tryouts that are held in the U.S. What Harley was offering was truly unusual. A new promotion paying well was offering the chance to work in the biggest arenas in Japan and was actively looking for new, fresh talent from the U.S. that didn't see the independent label as a stigma.

I thought about it and for a brief few days considered it. But it wasn't long before I talked myself out of it. I didn't see the fact that even if I tried out and didn't get picked, the experience was going to be a great lesson. I kept thinking of numerous excuses like I wasn't in ring shape, I hadn't wrestled in a while, and others. It was all bullshit. Here was a great world-class company I could put myself in front of to be seen by and I passed. Japan had always valued Mexican wrestlers and high flyer's as well as smaller wrestlers and paid them excellently, and yet I couldn't summon up the courage to put myself out there.

Ultimately, my friend Matt Murphy got picked to go as well as Superstar Steve. A few tours later Trevor Murdoch got his opportunity and even spent time training at the NOAH dojo and living in Japan for a period of time. They all deserved their tours as they had been consistent in their improvements and showed up ready for this great shot.

CHAPTER TWENTY-NINE
Layoff

For the next year, I put wrestling one-hundred percent on the back burner and it quickly forgot about me as well. No one called or asked me to work. I followed the sport through the Wrestling Observer website and watched it on TV.

In 2001, I took my first trip into the interior of Mexico with my best friend Miguel Saucedo. Mexico was a far more beautiful country than I could have ever imagined. We drove from Eagle Pass to Nuevo Laredo and crossed the border there to Monterrey. We drove all the way into Durango before resting for the night. The next day we drove through the treacherous Sicrra Madre mountains across the most winding harrowing road I had ever experienced before staying in the beach side town of Mazatlan.

We stayed in Mazatlan for several days while falling in love with the country as well as the city. The Mexican people treated us well, and it was empowering to be able to speak to everyone in Spanish. It would be one of our many trips together and separate exploring the country where our parents came from, but never really got to know and enjoy. Work was going well, and I was living a nice, comfortable life.

All of 2002 I was thinking wrestling was probably over. I never wrote it off, but I was enjoying all the things people who have regular hobbies do. I began to take classes at my local community collage. I started in a new area at work that required me to learn a new process and skills. I was enjoying being a home owner, having friends over, buying a pool table, and taking more vacations exploring Mexico.

I met a wonderful, Mexican girl from the state of Durango, Liliana. We kept a friendship over the phone and through occasional trips to Mexico. Talking on the phone with Liliana and my trips to Mexico forced me to improve my Spanish dramatically.

When I was in Mexico, I took in lucha libre matches every chance I had as a fan. They were interesting shows. I saw several in Monterrey, one in the border town of Matamaoros, and what appeared to be an independent show in Durango. The show in Durango was interesting in that the opening match was clearly two very young, inexperienced teenagers who may have been

139

having their very first match. Despite their obvious inexperience, they had great skills. They appeared to be very well trained with all their moves, and their conditioning was far better than many guys in the U.S. Indy scene with fifty or more matches under their belt.

It seemed that wrestling was possibly over for me. I began to hear stories through my two huge wrestling fan friends Derek Bates and Ray Rivera that the promoter I had met at our last show, Troy Peterson, was doing a lot of shows. Yet, I still continued with the attitude that, if he was interested in me, he knew who I was and obviously didn't want to use me. As I turned thirty, I pretty much knew I was getting too old without enough experience to ever be seriously considered for any prominent promotion even if I rededicated myself.

But in the summer of of 2003, I got a phone call out of the blue from the local sheriff's patrol. They were interested in holding a fundraiser and using wrestling as the attraction. I met with the head of the patrol, and they decided to put on a big show at Central Middle School in the beginning of October. They were interested in me booking the matches and helping find some retired AWA legends to appear and wrestle on the card.

CHAPTER THIRTY

Bockwinkel

The local sheriff's patrol wanted to promote a show called "Riverslam, An Evening With The Legends of Wrestling." With the help of Harley Race, I got Nick Bockwinkel's number and booked him as our former AWA legend. Nick gave me Mad Dog Vachon's phone number, and we booked him as well.

I talked to Travis Schillington and got some names for some talent we could book. He suggested a few people I hadn't worked with before such as Gage Octane and Johnny Fitness. I booked Lenny Lane and Scotty Zappa again, and we rounded out the card with the best midget wrestlers in the Midwest named Little Kato and Beautiful Bobby.

The highlight of the weekend was no doubt meeting the great Nick Bockwinkel. Nick was a second generation wrestler with his father Warren being a big star in the 1940's. Nick was a great athlete who played Division 1 football and had tremendous technical skills. In the 1970's he began wrestling in the AWA for Verne Gagne where he spent the majority of his career at and where he gained his biggest fame.

In the 1960's Ray Stevens was considered the best bump taker and in ring performer of that era. Stevens became the top star and biggest draw of the San Francisco territory where he also teamed with Pat Patterson. As the era of the 70's began, Stevens joined Gagne's territory and teamed with Bockwinkel. The two created one of the greatest tag teams of the 70's and really of all time. With Bobby Heenan in the corner, those two were heat seeking machines with the fans.

As the seventies progressed, Bockwinkel began focusing on his singles career more and becoming Verne Gagne's perennial top contender and opponent. He eventually got a run as AWA World Champion as Gagne, the aging owner of the company, dropped the belt to him. Then Bockwinkel was awarded the title one more time when Gagne retired in 1981.

Bockwinkel had a series of matches with the growing sensation of Hulk Hogan in the early 80's. Hogan started out as a bad guy, but his role in Rocky 3 as well as his undeniable charisma and stunning physique began to catch fire. Hogan developed into a more polished performer both in the ring with the incredible crew of talent the AWA had and in his interviews with the help of "Mean" Gene Okerlund and Gagne. Many people feel "Hulkamania" truly started in the AWA.

Gagne didn't want to give the title to the younger Hogan as he wasn't the pure wrestler he favored for his belt. Regardless, Nick and Hogan drew record gates in all the major cities the AWA ran in the Midwest as well as San Francisco and Denver.

When Hogan left, Nick spent the last few years of his career in the AWA. He dropped the belt in 1984 and then had one more run where he had a series of classic bouts against the future "Mr. Perfect" Curt Henning. Some of those matches were featured on national television on ESPN.

I was excited to meet Nick for dinner at Applebees with the organizer of the event. After the organizer left, Nick and I spoke for over two hours about his career in the business. He was gracious with his time and very generous.

When we were discussing the fact that it's so hard for wrestlers these days to learn when the locker rooms didn't have any veterans, he told me a great story of his days teaming with Stevens. Nick said, "We were somewhere up north, Fargo, I think. We had just finished the Main Event. Red Bastien was teaming with Wahoo, and it was the first time we were doing this match. It just didn't go great. It went okay, but it was nothing special. We all knew it needed to be better. So, here all four of us were trying to put our heads together, because we were not happy with the match. There were some young guys in the corner talking about what bar they were hitting that night or some other bullshit. I told them them they needed to be paying attention to what the hell was happening in front of them. If the four of us were not happy with it, they could learn something from what we were trying to figure out."

Can you imagine those four, four of the absolute greatest of their time, I mean all top guys with tons of experience at that time, and they were struggling with how to improve the match? The pride those guys had! What you'd learn listening as a fly on the wall!

Nick talked about how incredibly talented Bobby Heenan

was. He shared the same story with me that he did on the AWA DVD the WWE produced years later. "If someone couldn't make the town, Bobby would sometimes get in the ring and wrestle. He could do what me and Ray could do and get just as good of a reaction from the crowd. He could talk in interviews as well as us. He could do what we did plus what he did, but we couldn't do what he did!"

I was fascinated by the series of matches he had with the late Curt Henning. They were technical masterpieces with great wrestling and psychology, and they were often fifty to sixty minute matches! I always thought those matches subtly told a great story of the aging champion, who was past his prime, against the young challenger, who was still not quite in his prime, but you knew was on his way to be an all time great.

Nick shocked me when he told me he was fifty-three in 1987. The performances Nick showed in those incredible bouts really show his incredible athletic talents, conditioning, and pride he had as a wrestler. He kept up with Henning just as he was hitting his stride to becoming one of the best workers of his generation.

Bockwinkel talked about how great it was to work in the AWA during the 70's and early 80's when it was one of the premier territories. Unlike most promotions the wrestlers of the AWA only worked fifteen to twenty dates in a month. They were paid well as many of the cities they ran had good population bases. Also, Gagne had tremendous television in his areas, so consequently the promotion drew well. They also only ran many cities monthly rather than weekly. All this added up to a relatively mild travel schedule for a full-time wrestler. Gagne paid his talent well, so it was hard for many wrestlers who could handle the brutal Midwest winters to leave. Bockwinkel shocked me when he told me he actually bought a boat and had the time to use it recreationally. I had never heard a wrestler tell me about having the time to enjoy any type of hobby. The road was simply too demanding to allow for anything else.

Nick shared with me an insightful story of the character of Vince McMahon. When he decided to retire, Nick said he took a job as a road agent for McMahon. When he gave his notice to his

144

longtime rival, friend, and boss Verne Gagne, it was at his home over dinner. Gagne told him he would compete against McMahon and was willing to fight for his promotion. Nick said he advised Verne to sell or shut down. McMahon was a different breed of competitor. Not only was he ruthless, but he was also like the Terminator in his work pace. "His business is his hobby, his family, his legacy, his job, and his livelihood. How do you compete against someone like that?" questioned Nick. I thought about that as the years passed. How much energy do we put into our job? At least forty hours. How about our hobbies? I know I put many hours into my hobbies as most people do. Now add your legacy, your family, and how much time and energy are you putting into this endeavor?

As the night was finishing up, I asked Nick about Mil Mascaras. He was a favorite of mine when I was young, and Nick worked against him in Japan as well as the AWA. Mick Foley had buried Mil pretty thoroughly in his book as selfish, arrogant, and hard to work with. "Mil was one of the most handsome men I'd ever met, movie star good looks. I never understood why he wore a mask. My matches with Mil weren't as good as they should have been. Mil was a bit selfish in there. Of course, if you're not going to work hard to make me look good, how hard am I going to work to make you look good?"

After what seemed to be a half hour of talking, Nick said we better get going, so he could rest for Saturday night's show. I got up and looked around at the restaurant; we were the only people left! I was so engrossed in the stories of this legend I hadn't even realized the Applebees staff was busy wiping off tables and vacuuming the carpets all around us. It was almost midnight and closing time!

The next night we had a great night of wrestling. After over one year out of the ring, I gave myself the benefit of booking myself with a great mechanic in the ring named Gage Octane. I had Gage coming back later that night to do the tag match after one of our booked wrestlers couldn't make it. I gave him the win over the hometown boy to surprise the audience, but more importantly give him some additional heat for the tag.

Johnny Fitness and Dave Arrowood came down from Algona with Travis Schillington and wrestled the opener against T.S's new masked gimmick Thrillcat. Fitness was a jacked up blond, Algona native Trav trained for free, because he was a great athlete, a legit tough guy, and a big wrestling fan. Though Fitness was new and started wrestling late, in his 30's, it was obvious he was going to be very good and was going to be wrestling Main Events in the Indies right away.

Little Kato and Beautiful Bobby wrestled their outstanding Midget match. Nick Bockwinkel and Mad Dog Vachon signed autographs throughout the show and spoke before intermission. Vachon talked about the most popular wrestler in the history of Muscatine, The Crusher, calling him "one strong Polack!"

The tag match tore the house down. Trav and Gage Octane wrestled against Scotty Zappa and Mr. Destiny Jay Hanna, and they brawled throughout the entire building. They hit each other with chairs, trash cans, and just had the best match of the night having the crowd on its feet for half the battle.

Lenny finished the night with his Main Event that was good, but it was difficult to follow after the tag. It was poor booking on my part. We should have finished with the tag, since I wanted the guys in the tag to do some stuff outside and use some chairs.

I was hurting after the match due to me trying a tope to Gage outside the ring that missed him completely. I landed on my shoulder and it felt like I hurt it but didn't break anything. Despite the pain I was happy about the card. I'd gotten in the ring after a long layoff, and the match was actually pretty good. I didn't know what lay ahead, and I still had the bad attitude of waiting to see what was in store rather than making something happen. Yet, still at that time I was wondering if this might lead to something.

CHAPTER THIRTY-ONE

Black & Brave

After that fall show, nothing much happened until the following spring. I got a phone call from two brothers, Doug and Matt Ritter. Doug and Matt were from Muscatine as well and longtime fans. They had even helped us out one year setting up the ring. They had lent me a Dusty Rhodes shoot interview and had always been friendly with me whenever we ran into each other.

Turned out the brothers had become super fans traveling the Midwest watching Indy shows with a variety of talent especially Ian Rottens IWA Mid-South. They were preparing to promote their very first show and were interested in booking me. I was grateful for the chance and said yes. They had me pegged to work the opening match against someone I'd never heard of, "Snake Eyes" Mike Andrews, but I didn't mind. As inactive as I'd been, I was becoming someone no one had ever heard of quickly.

The card was in nearby Rock Island, Illinois, on March 28, 2004. I got to the show early as I hoped to get in the ring and do a couple spots with the guy I was working with. When I got there, there were two very young guys, teenagers, working out in the ring. They hadn't been trained yet they told me, but their work was very good and smooth. You could tell they were heavily influenced by the new Ring Of Honor promotion that had just begun in the Northeast appealing to Internet savvy fans who appreciated a faster-paced, athletic style of wrestling.

They were very nice and polite as I talked to them a bit. Both had lean physiques and still looked so young, but were still impressive. It turned out they were part of a backyard promotion that had its own ring, Scott County Wrestling. However, the pair didn't wrestle like any backyard wrestlers I had ever met. I would meet them along the way of my continued journey in wrestling. Within a few matches and with some training, they would go on and wrestle on the Indy scene as Tyler Black and Marek Brave. Black would eventually become today's WWE Superstar Seth Rollins.

I thought about asking them where they trained and how often. I figured that even as good as they were there were some things I could help them with. I'd never had access to a ring anywhere nearby, so it was great opportunity to work out with some hungry, young guys. But of course I never saw opportunities as clearly then as I see them now, so I didn't say anything more than make some small talk with them and comment that their work was good.

My match with Andrews was pretty uneventful. The locker room was anything but that. The card didn't have a single person I knew on it, a first for me really. It was amazing how quickly the business had changed in the short time I'd been away. Austin Aries was in the Main Event against Danny Daniels. Aries was becoming a top guy in the Midwest. I was interested in seeing him in the ring after the buzz he was getting. He wasn't very tall, a little shorter than me, but he was a small-framed guy who had packed as much muscle as he could on his frame.

As the Main Event came up, most of the guys found a spot where we could view the match. Aries was as good as his reputation. Explosive was the term that came to mind. He had a unique, believable, athletic style that was just in your face. It was innovative at the time as well. He could mat wrestle as well as perform the high flying moves hardcore fans loved to see on the independent scene. Daniels kept up with Aries and they had a great physical match. Daniels won the match, because Aries said in the locker room he was making plans to move to the Philadelphia area to work for ROH.

After the card the Ritter's asked me if I'd come back in April for their next card, and I gladly agreed to it. I knew I wasn't going to be an important part of their promotion, but I was glad to be in a locker room with some top Indy talent and just glad to be back in the ring.

CHAPTER THIRTY-TWO

No Limits Wrestling

My next show for the Ritter's promotion of No Limits Wrestling was May 14th. I was booked in a three way tag team match with Tony Rican as my partner. Tony was from Chicago and a high flyer who had worked against our opponents, so I got a spot in for me during the babyface part of the shine. Since we were going to be eliminated first, I pretty much had a night off.

The locker room was again an eclectic group of Midwest independent wrestlers. Just to give some serious wrestling fans an idea of the card in the opening match, they had Shawn Daivari vs Petey Williams.

Daivari was another young Minnesota guy who was developing a name for himself. He had wrestled against Aries countless times and had a creative finisher where he utilized his Arabic heritage. "The Magic Carpet" was a top rope splash that Daivari used with a colorful Middle East carpet spread out as he landed on his opponent.

Williams walked in after a long drive from Canada just about an hour before the bell time. After they shook hands, Williams asked Daivari if he'd ever seen his finisher, "The Canadian Destroyer." Daivari shook his head no. I hadn't either, so I listened curiously. Williams described what seemed to be a reverse pile driver. Williams described his unique, dangerous sounding finisher and told Daivari that although he'd never hurt anyone with it, he'd understand if Daivari didn't want to take it. Williams understood, because they hadn't ever worked together before. Daivari respectfully said he'd rather not do the finisher, having never seen it or had a chance to practice it. Williams said no problem and they came up with another finish. Petey Williams would take that move to TNA and make a career out of it along with his in ring work.

Daivari would be signed by the WWE that summer and rocketed to the main roster because of his ability to speak Persian. Soon he was at Wrestlemania being thrown around by Hulk Hogan. But right now he was just paying his dues traveling around and having great matches.

Jimmy Jacobs would wrestle Ian Rotten in the middle of the card. Jacobs was a smaller guy who started very young in

Michigan and had traveled anywhere he could to get experience. He had a lot of charisma, but he was going to have an uphill battle in an industry that was always looking for the next guy who was tall and over 240 pounds. Rotten was an aging, beat-up veteran wrestler who had worked in Texas at the Sportatorium for a time when he was young. He made a splash in the ECW (Extreme Championship Wrestling) having horribly violent, bloody matches. He promoted matches under his own IWA Mid-South banner, and it was a place many young wrestler with ambition went to get work. It had a cult following both in its home base of Indiana and selling D.V.D.'s on the Internet.

Seeing Ian and talking to him was sometimes painful. As cruel as it sounds, he was what I most feared of becoming in the wrestling business. A guy who gave it everything he had, including his health and his finances but didn't have the talent, the genetics, the discipline or get the breaks to ever make a good living off of it.

There was a guy in the back who was preparing for his match against Arik Cannon who kept going over chain wrestling moves in his head. His name was Chris Hero. He was a tall guy with long, brown hair. Hero would later get a WWE contract and was doing well in NXT before he was let go.

It was also the first time I would meet Colt Cabana. Cabana was a young guy from Chicago who was about six feet tall with a solid build, though he wasn't very muscular. He was a guy who liked to have fun, always joking around and smiling. When they stuck a microphone in front of him, he cut a tremendous promo with references to wrestling history that made it clear he was a student of the game. Cabana made it a point to talk to me and asked me how it felt to be the only one in the locker room who didn't know anybody. I told him I was cool with it, and I really was as everyone was very easy to be around.

When Cabana went out to his entrance music of "Copacabana" from Barry Manilow, it really was great. The crowd loved it and he certainly had charisma. He was a polished performer for being so young. His match with Brad Bradley was excellent and had great crowd interaction.

The main event was TNA star A.J. Styles. Styles was a class act. He was about my height, but he was in great shape. He was lean but not skinny. He was from Georgia, so he had the southern accent to go along with the nice manners. Styles was becoming the face of TNA, the new promotion started by Jeff Jarrett and his father, legendary Tennessee promoter, Jerry Jarrett. He had great athletic skills and seemed to be the wrestler that many of these new independent wrestlers I was meeting were trying to become. He was a hybrid wrestler who could work any Japanese and Mexican star in their style.

Once again as the main event started, every single guy on the card got a spot in the back of the stands and watched. They were not going to miss a match with one of the best wrestlers in the U.S. to see what they could learn. All these guys on the card seemed to have so much passion for wrestling. It was occurring to me that here was a group of guys who frankly loved it even more than I did, something I would have considered unfathomable a few years ago. They lived for the weekend to wrestle. They wanted to work every single Friday, Saturday, and Sunday if possible. They talked only about wrestling and drove long miles in cars full of others like them. None of them brought girlfriends along. They didn't have other careers, hobbies, or goals that didn't involve wrestling. They wanted to be around other like-minded people, the only ones that understood them.

Styles worked a tremendous match against Danny Daniels. He showed why he was where he was. He and this card showed me there was a group of young wrestlers out here who had set up their lives to have one priority, wrestling. They had passed me up through their number of matches. Just like Lenny Lane and the Tony Robbins principle, it wasn't the years but the amount of matches that mattered. If I'd stayed in Texas and worked in the CWA at the Sportatorium alongside all those great veterans like Johnny Mantell and Sam Houston, I would have something to offer that these young guys could never get at this level.

Because I hadn't, if I wanted to get better I would have to start almost new. But I had some things going for me. I'd been trained right and I *had* worked in the Sportatorium and been around

153

some true legends and great minds. I had sat and listened to Grizzly Smith and Skandar Akbar talk for hours. I also was finally becoming the student of the game I needed to be to do anything at all even if it was just on the Indy scene. Technology was making things easier as interviews with wrestlers were becoming available where they would sometimes drop tidbits of information on the craft. Print interviews were being done with the great performers and minds of the business on what worked, what didn't, and why. Books were becoming more common with a few lessons in the pages on the craft. A craft that had been kept secret for decades and guarded obsessively was slowly opening up its history and insights on what made a great performer great. I needed a canvas to try these insights I'd read and picked up the last few years while on the sidelines.

CHAPTER THIRTY-THREE

Heel

I gratefully worked a few more shows for the Ritter brothers. As the summer ended in 2004, I got a phone call at my house from Troy Peterson, the owner and promoter of Impact Pro Wrestling. Troy had been doing some shows out of Delta, Iowa, monthly as well as spot shows all over Iowa and a few in Minnesota.

He called to see if I'd be interested in working for IPW on the next Delta show scheduled for September. We talked for over an hour and hit it off right away. I agreed to wrestle on the next card and was interested in seeing what Delta, Iowa, was all about. I had talked with my friend Derek Bates a bit about the stuff he'd seen on message boards. Derek said it sounded like they were running angles, had a hot crowd, and were drawing well.

When I talked with Troy, he didn't have anything in mind as far as a match or opponent. I think he mentioned me working heel which was something I was interested in seeing if I could pull off. I'd never really been given the chance to be a heel. Harley Race booked me once as a heel against Matt Murphy, but it was only one show in front of a crowd of strangers who I had never been in front of and was never going to see again. I didn't get to cut a promo or give any ideas for what I'd do. Truth was I'd never been asked for any ideas and understandably so. I was green, my look and normal behavior all said vanilla babyface.

Though over the years I'd thought a heel Mexican character would get over. I thought a guy coming out cutting a promo in Spanish and adding in English how ignorant all the small town rednecks were would get real organic heat. I knew how much even the most non-racist whites resented immigrants who didn't learn English. They also didn't like people speaking Spanish around them. They were always paranoid we were speaking about them.

I had many of my friends at work tell me they had no problems with Hispanics like me who were proud of our heritage, but they didn't like Latinos who flew their native flag in their front lawn. They didn't like seeing Mexican flags on bumper stickers. They would sincerely ask me, "If they love Mexico so much, Juan, why did they leave?" I knew I needed to bring my

Mexican flag to the ring.

I had read in Mick Foley's book that Micheal Hayes told him, "A heel needs to feel justified." As a heel I had many reasons to feel justified in my words and actions. All a wrestling persona or character is supposed to be is you with the volume turned up. A larger than life version of who you really are.

I am a very proud Mexican American who is very thankful my parents insisted I retain my Spanish. I get annoyed when we Americans get upset when people are using a language other than English to communicate. I knew from traveling in Mexico and talking to friends from the Philippines, South America, and all over the world that the one language everyone is trying to learn is English. There was no threat of any language taking over more than English.

It also broke my heart to hear so many stories from Mexicans when I traveled there of how they in fact loved Mexico, but the economic opportunities there were so small that they longed to come to America. That was why the ones who did immigrate to the U.S. still had a deep affection for Mexico, just not for its politicians.

Also, many people in Iowa have been so far removed from the immigrant experience that they lost sympathy for those who come to this country and are struggling with the language and traditions. All that just takes time. Since many don't have a grandparent they can remember who spoke with an accent, they can't understand how much time it takes to become assimilated. Often it's as simple as the children of immigrants becoming fully immersed in the culture and language; it takes time.

All this added up to me in real life being able to grab that part of me that was so proud of my Mexican roots and turn it way up. All the while I turned off the part of me that understood people's opposing points of view. I was proud of my family's service to this country dating back to my mom's uncle who served in World War II.

All this sounded great on paper, but I hadn't mentioned any of this to Troy. They were ideas I'd had for some time but never had an opportunity to use. When I showed up in Delta, I shook hands and met some new faces. I also learned Travis Schillington had not only been wrestling for Troy and supplying the ring for IPW, he'd become Troy's right hand man, his lieutenant. He helped with booking, finishes, and running the locker room.

Troy made me feel welcome and right at home. When he and Trav talked to me, they said I'd be wrestling the opening match against Trav in his gimmick of Thrillcat. Troy and Trav asked me if I had any ideas on my gimmick as a heel. I told them about my Mexican flag and my ideas of being an anti-American heel. I talked about my idea of cutting a promo in Spanish and then switching into English. Troy thought for a second and said it was way better than anything he had. He told me to do that, all of it. He told me to go ahead and get on the mic and cut the promo also.

For the very first time in my life, a promoter asked me for my ideas. The best part was this guy didn't even hesitate; he just gave me the green light. It sounded good to him. I'd read about the great Bill Watts taking talents' ideas all the time. It didn't matter to Watts who's idea it was. Watts said he always felt that no one knew better than the talent themselves about their character. Paul Heyman did that in the ECW to great success, letting talent come up with some of their own angles, gimmicks, and finishes. The only thing that mattered was what was best for business.

Most Indy promoters at the time would have balked at giving a guy they'd never booked a chance to cut a promo. But over and over the history of the business shows talents have to have input on their characters in order for it to succeed.

Trav and I talked over an outline for a very basic match. When I went out to the ring to the sound of my Spanish music, I got a lot of neutral reactions as it was my debut in the small, rural town of Delta, population 328. As soon as I held up my Mexican flag, that all changed. When I picked up the microphone, it really changed.

"Yo estoy aqui por una rason y una rason solamente. Para ensenarle a todos usteded qui la styla lucha libre Mexicana es mucnho mas mehor de la styla Americano! Oh, I forgot. I'm in Delta, Iowa, home of a bunch of redneck Iowa pig farmers. See, unlike you people, I speak two languages, dos idiomas!" I finished up my anti-American promo promising victory and gave the mic back to Steve Shettler, the ring announcer.

It was instant feedback, and it was good. A chorus of boos rained on me and the chants of "U.S.A., U.S.A., U.S.A." filled the Delta Dome. I was a true heel. No one was cheering me, just what I wanted. It was a visceral reaction from this small town, born in the U.S.A. crowd, they didn't like me.

Thrillcat came out waving an American flag and the crowd was into our match! We had a basic good guy vs bad guy match, and the audience was involved the whole time. When Thrillcat pinned me after a ten minute bout and the crowd popped, I felt a deep sense of satisfaction. I was a heel.

When we got to the back, Troy said he loved it. The other wrestlers in the locker room such as Johnny Fitness and Mr. Destiny Jay Hanna congratulated us on the reaction we got. Troy immediately told me I was booked for the next shows in Delta.

On the drive home, I was feeling great   After all these years, I'd found a promoter who gave me a chance to try being a heel with this character. Delta was only eighty miles from my house, and Troy paid well. Here was a venue I could do angles at and I could come back every month to see what was working and what didn't. I'd get a chance to cut promos, something I never really had done. The crowd was a great wrestling crowd, loud and enthusiastic. I had found my canvas and my laboratory to try the concepts and principles I'd been studying the past couple years from the sidelines.

CHAPTER THIRTY-FOUR

Troy Peterson

In my time off, I had spent my time reading books about the art of professional wrestling, the craft. Another great resource that began to become prevalent was "shoot interviews." Pioneered by R.F. Video, they were interviews with legends of the business talking about their careers. These videos ran the gamut of how these veterans broke into wrestling, who influenced them, their relationships with different promoters and other talent, as well as the territories they worked over their career.

In any other business or craft, these resources would be readily available at your local library, bookstore, or clubs. For example, when I decided to become a landlord and buy my first rental property in my plant alone there were a dozen landlords who I could quiz. In town there was a local landlord association and numerous books available in my library. However, in wrestling due to the secretive nature of the business throughout its lifetime much of its history, knowledge, and information was not readily available.

In the old days, the information was passed slowly through a guy working night after night. Driving with veterans was another key aspect of learning the craft. After the card on the drive to the next town or home, the veterans picked apart your work and told you what you did right and what you did wrong. This continued year after year and in different territories in different parts of the country, so you became a very well-rounded talent if you paid attention.

But now that the territories were dead, you didn't have those great opportunities to ever learn from those wise, old veterans. These shoot videos would sometimes contain small bits of information that were golden. Angles that had been done in parts of the country you never had seen, because you didn't get that TV station when you were growing up.

For example, in Dusty Rhodes R.F. Video shoot he said that what made Nikita Koloff successful was what made the original Sheik a top guy, he lived his gimmick. He said Nikita walked around Charlotte speaking with a Russian accent all the time despite being from Minnesota. People said, "That guy is from

Russia!" So, the people believed in him and that made his gimmick be that much more over.

I began to learn that almost nothing in wrestling is original. Most great angles have been copied over the years. But if a fan sitting in the stands has never seen or heard of it, it's new to them and that's all that matters.

I saw a great shoot interview with the late Eddie Gilbert. Gilbert was a great booker and antagonist who helped influence Paul Heyman early on. Despite being in his 20's, Bill Watts allowed him to book his territory for a period of time. In the interview, he described a fantastic angle he did in Mid-South that involved him as a manager of a Russian villain in the mid 80's at the height of the Cold War. On TV he apologized to the owner wrestling legend "Cowboy" Bill Watts over ever associating himself with a Russian and vowed he would no longer do that.

With the Soviet flag in hand, he handed it to Watts who suggested they burn it and promised he would never manage the evil Russian again. As Watts accepted his apology and they made amends, Eddie Gilbert double-crossed Watts and a trio of Russian wrestlers attacked Watts along with Eddie Gilbert. They did a number on him and busted him open. With Watts a bloody mess from being attacked by all three Russians, Gilbert grabbed the Red Soviet flag and draped it over the body of the proud American Patriot Bill Watts. In the background the great Jim Ross and Micheal Hayes, one of the most underrated announcing teams in history, were going ballistic selling the angle.

I thought the segment was tremendous and the heat it generated with fans was great. I was talking with Troy Peterson one night about the upcoming Delta show, and we were coming up with ideas for my match with Vin Cross. I suggested a match with Cory where I get the victory after cheating and put a beating on him after the match. After laying him out, I proposed draping the Mexican flag over Cory just as Gilbert did in that great angle. The following month we could do a flag match as the rubber match where I lose.

Once again Troy gave the angle the green light. We were talking for hours on the phone about wrestling, wrestling, and more wrestling. Troy was my age and was a rare promoter who not only didn't wrestle, he had no desire to ever wrestle, manage, or be involved in angles. That was such a throwback to those successful promoters such as Jim Crockett who were true businessman interested in what was best for the promotion and the fans.

Troy gave me the most valuable commodity any wrestler must have, confidence. If you don't have confidence, you're never going to have any success in wrestling. Also, it does help to have someone give you some positive feedback on your talent and work. Troy was the very first promoter I knew, especially someone our age or younger, who truly looked at it from a fan's perspective. While he could appreciate the talent of a great "worker" or technical wrestler in the ring, he wasn't afraid to call a boring wrestler boring. I remember him saying in the locker room that one of the most respected talents whom everyone, myself included, raved about was never going to be in the main event in Delta. He said, "Nobody cares about him. The fans don't care about him."

The most popular wrestler with the fans in Delta was Johnny Fitness, Dave Arrowood. Dave was a good-looking, blond haired guy with a fantastic build. He had tons of charisma, was a great athlete, and was popular with all types of fans. Naturally, the women and teenage girls liked him. Yet, he was not only admired by the women. The teenage boys thought his strength and physique were awesome, and the men appreciated his toughness and athletic ability.

However, a few guys in the locker room resented Dave, because he was relatively inexperienced. He was was still green when he got put in Main Events right away although by that point he was up to speed with his ring work. Some guys felt the best worker deserved some of those spots. Frankly, I'd been taught that also at times. Troy was the first promoter to explain that was bullshit. Were the Road Warriors green as shit when they debuted in Georgia Championship Wrestling? Sure, but we both thought they were awesome! We were pure fans then and thought the face paint, physiques, and intensity of these guys were incredible! How about my favorite wrestler as a teen, the Ultimate Warrior? Same thing! I loved him even though his ring work wasn't always the best. It didn't matter! He sold tickets and merchandise and I loved the guy! I cared about him.

Troy didn't care that Dave wasn't trained x amount of months before his first match. He didn't care that Dave didn't pay his dues before being put into his first Main Events. Troy said, "Dave paid his dues traveling with Trav. Learning on those drives and helping set up the ring. Dave paid his dues in the gym." When Troy told me that, I remembered The Ultimate Warrior in a press conference saying he didn't have to do things other wrestlers did in order to be successful, "I don't do arm drags or hip tosses. I pay my dues in the gym and with my intensity." I'd forgotten that lesson I had learned as a fan until Troy reminded me.

Another exciting thing happening in IPW was their training school having a great camp with several talented new young wrestlers who showed promise right from the start. One of the trainees was Matt Ferguson. He was a classic, young babyface who reminded me of Tommy "Wildfire" Rich. The girls loved his youthful looks, and the rest of the fans liked the fire he showed in the ring. The other standout of the camp was Juan Areola or as we named him Montoya X. Montoya was a great athlete, explosive, with a tremendous frog splash off the top rope that really got some air time. Montoya had good size at around six foot tall and was an athletic-looking 240 pounds. The rest of the camp showed some promise as well, especially Danny Wagner and Anthony Sieren.

As the next Delta date approached, I decided that I was going to try to live my gimmick the way Dusty Rhodes said Nikita Koloff did in the Carolinas. It wasn't that big of a sacrifice being that Delta was ninety miles away. Plus it was only one day a month, but I was going to be a heel, a real heel. I was not going to mingle or fraternize with the fans during intermission or after the show. I wasn't going to try to be the cool heel, no autographs or pictures with the fans either. If the boys went out after the card to the local bar, I wasn't going. I was not going to give the fans a chance to see me be Juan, the polite Midwesterner who had more in common with them than not.

Vin Cross was a good heel who was turned babyface and wasn't the best fit for the role. But I thought it would be a great challenge to try to get the fans solidly behind Vin Cross to see if my character was as successful a heel as I hoped. As we went out for the match, our big goal was to execute the angle after the finish to set up the flag match for next month.

When I went out for my promo before the match, I got an even stronger reaction than the month before. The crowd was a bit bigger and now knew my character, so I wasn't too surprised. When Vin Cross came out, they cheered him as simply the guy who they hoped would beat me. They did not necessarily cheer him as their hero.

We locked up and had a good solid bout with some solid wrestling and action. When he made his comeback, I remembered those lessons I'd learned over the past few years of what a heel is supposed to be. Stone Cold Steve Austin said he felt a wrestler could not be a great heel unless he was a bumping heel. When I read that I thought about the amazing heat that Kamikaze Kid would get in his matches consistently. When the babyface he was beating up finally made his comeback, Kamikaze told me over the phone once that the heel's job is to bump "all over the fucking ring for the babyface." I saw this over and over when I studied the great heels of the modern era like Rick Rude, Ric Flair, Curt Henning, Shawn Michaels, and Austin before his body broke down. So, now I knew what my job was when Vin Cross started his comeback, bump. Take big bumps and get right back up for more bumps; take outlandish bumps if I could safely.

These were not intricate lessons, bump big for your babyface in his comeback. Live your gimmick. They were wrestling 101 in many cases, the fundamentals. But what I was learning was that many people on the Indy scene never master the fundamentals or even use them. Just by following these basic principles, I was becoming a good heel in Delta. One who got heat, one that people cared about, and one they wanted to see get his ass

165

kicked.

I won the match by cheating and then attacked him after the bell as well. Just as we planned, I grabbed my Mexican flag and held it up parading around the ring. I took the flag and draped it over his face and upper body leaving him in the ring to some good heat from the small-town Delta crowd.

When Vin Cross came to, he grabbed the Mexican flag, got on the mic, and challenged me to a flag match the next month at the Delta Dome. The angle worked perfectly. I didn't feel bad one bit stealing a great angle from some of the most talented minds in the history of wrestling. That is a wonderful part of the business, imitation really is the sincerest form of flattery. I was using the time I spent outside the ring studying the business. As I was learning, those old principles still worked. Since I was a guy in Iowa who had been trained in Texas, I had a slightly different view of things, a different set of knowledge from watching old Mid-South TV and Georgia Championship Wrestling on TBS. Many of the guys in the Delta locker room were younger and only knew the modern product of WWE and WCW. I was also simply at a stage in life, 31, when you realize you don't know as much as you thought. You begin to really pay attention to the guys who have been successful in whatever industry you're studying.

We came back to Delta the next month and had the blow off to the angle we did with Vin Cross, a flag match. It was explained to the crowd that the loser of the match would be required to salute the winner's national flag.

One added element we had going into the match was having Montoya X second me to the ring. Being a young new heel and of Mexican descent, it made sense to have him accompany me. We also were planning a few shows ahead trying to set up a feud that would utilize Montoya and Matty Starr, the new students, in a feud with me and Johnny Fitness.

As we started the match, I could tell I had some real heat. The fans really wanted me to lose, but weren't sure this was the guy who could pull it off. They also didn't want to see their babyface have to salute the Mexican flag.

166

As we came up to the finish, Montoya interfered and it backfired costing me the victory. As Vin Cross pinned me, the pop from the Delta crowd was "sickening" according to Johnny Fitness. I had done my job and the pop from the crowd as I was forced to salute the American flag was my applause.

CHAPTER THIRTY-FIVE
I.P.W.

Delta was really a great time in my career. As I faced off with Johnny Fitness in a series of angles, Troy and I were able to collaborate with each other over the phone. We bounced off ideas we had and angles we loved.

Once again I grabbed an old angle from Mid-South and blatantly stole it. In the mid 80s, Chavo and Hector Guerrero were feuding against the Rock & Roll Express. The Guerreros were the heels dressed in their sombreros and bandit outfits speaking Spanish and accusing Mid-South of discriminating against them because they were Mexican. They even went so far as to insist they wanted a Mexican referee in order for things to be fair.

I thought that was great, so I asked Troy to allow me to use Ray Gomez, a Puerto Rican aspiring wrestler from Muscatine, as a referee. Montoya and I copied the Guerrero angle by saying in order to be fair we needed a Latino referee.

Ray was great in his role and, when he blatantly turned against the babyfaces allowing us to get our win, he also got great heat. When we were leaving the ring, we had several fans get awfully close to us, especially Ray, threatening us. They called us plenty of racial epitaphs, but I felt that was just part of getting real heat. I pulled out of Delta one time and actually had kids throw rocks at my truck.

As much heat as I got, I knew it wasn't anything close to the heat Skandar Akbar got in New Orleans. He regularly got his tires slashed and one night had to wear a bulletproof vest in the Superdome. Another time irate fans threw Liquid Drano into his eyes, blinding him for a few days.

As we finished up my first year in Delta, we led up to a hair vs hair match with Johnny Fitness. It was a good match that got a lot of praise from the locker room. I lost the match getting my hair buzzed off in patches before I fled the ring.

It was a great year for me in Delta and with IPW. I finally found a promoter and promotion who liked me and offered me the chance to be on all their shows. My wrestling career felt

169

revived.

I got enough enthusiasm for wrestling again that I decided to promote another hometown show. We booked Perry Saturn for the main event against the 275 pound monster Mr. Destiny Jay Hanna. I wrestled second match against Gage Octane in a rematch from our River Slam event. We had a loud, enthusiastic crowd fill the armory in town. As I waited for my entrance music to hit for the first time, I heard my hometown crowd loudly chanting, "Thunder, Thunder!" It was a great feeling as I went to the ring. Gage made me look like a million bucks and I got my win.

After intermission Troy, Travis, and Jay asked me what we were going to do about Perry Saturn as he still hadn't showed up. We hadn't heard a word from him either; we were getting nervous. Perry had made all the dates for Troy in Delta and other towns, so we weren't sure what the problem was.

Troy got a hold of Sonny Ono, Perry's manager for bookings at the time. Sonny didn't have a clue where Perry was. Soon after, Troy got a call from Perry. Perry said he had been in a car accident and couldn't make the show.

We were in a bad spot. I had always booked name talent who I felt confident would be reliable such as One Man Gang, Nick Bockwinkell, Lenny Lane, and others. In some cases circumstances couldn't be avoided, such as when we booked "Cowboy" Bob Orton out of St. Louis for a show and he got injured. We quickly were able to replace him with Marty Jannetty and had a great turnout.

Now we had advertised someone with every reason to believe they would make the shot and something out of our control intervened. Troy, Travis, and Jay were all in agreement that the only option was for me to come back and wrestle Jay in the main event. There was one match after intermission which was ending, Travis vs his pupil Matty Starr, aka Matt Ferguson. We had to make a decision.

I knew in my gut what they were saying was right, but I still hadn't worked a main event match at that point. I knew a main event should have a big fight feel, be special and different than anything else on the card. I pushed away my doubts about being in the main event as I knew everyone was right, it was our only option. Travis told us as he headed out the door for his match that they would go as long as they could to give me and Destiny some more time to quickly put together our match.

Jay and I figured out a basic layout of the match with selling him as the very believable monster he was and me being the underdog, undersized hometown guy going against a very real threat who I more than likely couldn't beat.

Trav and Matty did their part well by having a fantastic veteran heel against the young babyface match. They used all kinds of old-school techniques to get the crowd, especially the kids, behind Matty before Trav got the win through interference.

Jay walked out to the ring and cut a promo saying Perry Saturn was afraid of him and he was going to beat someone up regardless and running down Muscatine. When I appeared the crowd was behind me, but they were also disappointed to see Perry Saturn really wasn't there. I cut a promo saying we had always delivered on our bookings, but this was out of our control and I apologized to the fans. I then told Destiny if he wanted a match I was ready for one.

We had a good main event that felt like a big fight. The match had legitimate tension and heat with the real-life story that had played out with Saturn no showing and this unexpected match happening. I felt we had delivered and Jay came up with a good finish that had me hurricanrana out of a power bomb for a quick pin where I bolted out of the ring right after the three count from referee Billy Jay.

I just kept feeling as though I was growing as a wrestler, developing, and making progress. Working a main event match and delivering was an important step for my confidence. I was ready to network and try a few other bookings again outside of IPW.

CHAPTER THIRTY-SIX
Lucha

At this point in time, I was starting to read message boards and was intrigued by the lucha libre shows being run in Chicago. There seemed to be a few promotions bringing in some top talent from Mexico with most of the under card being supplied by older Mexican locals.

I contacted one of the promoters who ran regularly. He quickly responded to my e mail and booked me for his next show in the Chicago suburb of Aurora. The show drew a smaller crowd of 150 people or so, mainly Mexican immigrants.

The show was fascinating to work on though, since it was the first time I'd been booked on a lucha card. The headliner for the show was Heavy Metal. His brother was a Mexican legend, Negro Casas, and his father was the famous Mexican referee Pepe Casas. Metal looked trim and fit. He was an outstanding wrestler in his own right as I saw him wrestle on the Mexican television station of Galavision which I had started to watch regularly on Sunday afternoons. He was very accommodating in the back with the promoter saying he was willing to do whatever he needed as there were some last minute changes in the card. I figured he was getting a great payday and was eager to make the Chicago promoter happy, so he could continue these bookings.

The older guys on the card were all very nice to me. I was a bit worried how I'd be treated, but I walked in with the attitude of being thankful for the booking and eager to learn something. All the older guys welcomed me to sit with them as they all spoke in Spanish. My Spanish had improved to the point that this situation didn't terrify me like it would have five years before.

I learned all these guys in the locker room were in their mid forties and one, Beto, was even older. They had been full-time lucha wrestlers in Mexico in their younger years. They had been trained in lucha in different parts of Mexico. When the work dried up either through age or simply less and less live cards being run, they immigrated to the U.S.

They all resided in the Chicago area, worked a variety of factory jobs, and lived a very typical Mexican immigrant experience. Chicago has a huge Mexican population and I could see the appeal of living there if you were an immigrant. You could find great food and Mexican neighborhoods to ease the pain of missing home. O'Hare had daily direct flights to Mexico and the best entertainment in Mexico regularly came to Chicago to perform. Plus Chicago with its large Polish and other ethnic communities understood the immigrant experience well.

I was paired up in a tag match with one of the older veterans who wrestled as Sagittarius under a mask. We worked against another lucha veteran and an American Indy worker. The match went well and Sagittarius did a great looking tope, a flying dive, from the top rope to his opponent on the floor. It was an amazing spot considering Sagittarius' age and he weighed about 230 pounds.

When we got to the back, Sagittarius told the promoter Jose I could work and suggested he book me again. Most of the guys were impressed by my size. I was only five foot nine and weighed 215 pounds at the time. However, I'd been hitting the weights good and, with it being mainly a Mexican locker room with older vets, I was both taller than most of them and had the most athletic physique there. It was something that had slowly been changing everywhere on the Indy scene. When I had walked into the Sportatorium, I was the smallest guy in the locker room at 205 pounds. Slowly smaller guys began to fill the locker room as well as, unfortunately, more people who didn't go the gym. Even on a good Indy card, I was always going to be a decent-sized guy.

One of the Chicago lucha guys was named Luis and he was working the main. He amazed me by sitting in our locker room the whole night while slowly drinking his beer and conversing about everything under the sun. As the second to last match started, he said in Spanish, "Well, guys, I probably should go into the other locker room and see what we're doing in the match."

I walked out to see the main along with Sagittarius. When the match started, I couldn't believe Luis work. He was doing lucha exchanges flawlessly before he tagged out. When his partner Black Tiger stepped in, the other guy tagged in Heavy Metal. Sagittarius whispered to me, "Watch these guys work, bro." Sure enough they put on a clinic in lucha. Back and forth holds and

174

counters, pin attempts were all done so smoothly. They were pros, well trained with thousands of hours of experience in front of crowds with good opponents as well as tours of Japan. They were world-class wrestlers.

I learned in the locker room and from Sagittarius next to me that what they called that was "el basico," the basics. All luchadores got el basico drilled into their head in training and in the arenas all over Mexico. It was basically the fundamentals of lucha, and they all could do it smoothly without talking about anything beforehand.

The Mexican vets had told me of their struggle to become wrestlers in Mexico. They were all guys from modest and often poor backgrounds. Finding the money to train was very difficult. Most of them couldn't gain sufficient weight to be considered for training. Unlike me they didn't have access to all the protein they could eat. I had a great gym only four blocks down from me and my dad paid the twenty-two dollar yearly membership. They had no access to good training programs and only had expensive run-down, poorly-equipped gyms to train at. They made their own horrible concoctions of weight-gain shakes made up of raw eggs while I had my good-tasting shakes from G.N.C.

When they finally got into a training camp, they trained six days a week and not the once or twice a week most of us did. They trained for six to nine months for four to six hours a day. When they made it through camp, they had to have a sponsor or "padrino" take them in front of the local wrestling commission. The commission was made up of ex wrestlers, referees, and respected veterans. If you didn't know how to work, if you couldn't do "el basico," you didn't get your license. I began to understand why even the greenest young wrestler I saw in Mexico working the opening match was so good at the fundamentals.

After the great main event, I thanked the promoter Jose and told him I'd love to work again. Luis invited me to train at their warehouse they would work out in on Sundays. I told him I would do that and I was interested in learning a little lucha to use in my matches.

The training sessions in Chicago were helpful in just learning a few drills and a few lucha spots I could use in my matches. That was something One Man Gang had encouraged even back when I promoted my first show. I made about five sessions before the group lost their warehouse to train in.

The most fun opportunity to come out of the contacts I'd made with Jose the promotor was a Lucha Va Voom show that was being promoted on Cinco De Mayo in 2006. These shows have grown into huge hip events in Los Angeles and other big cities today. At that time they were beginning to gain some steam as fun shows that combined of all things Burlesque and lucha libre masked wrestling!

Jose the promoter had the task of providing talent for the opening Battle Royal match. The pay was fifty dollars and the show was going to be fun and interesting, so I jumped all over it.

The agent handling the matches in the back had us all line up in our gear and proceeded to decide in what order we would be eliminated. Despite not having a mask or flashy gear, he had me going out near the end. After I was eliminated, there would be two guys left to decide the winner. I was happy with the spot and ready to enjoy the night after our Battle Royal ended. We had an added bonus of having ring girls accompany us during our entrance.

I was in Chicago in a cool, old venue, The Congress Theater. The crowd was hot as it was Cinco de Mayo and a Thursday night, I believe. The crowd was very unique. It was full of young hipsters, professionals, and a mainly white audience. Many of the girls in the audience were wearing their lucha masks while sipping on their drinks in their stylish clothing. The crowd was large, around a thousand, maybe more. The event had a real sponsor, El Jimador Tequila. A fantastic tequila I'd fallen in love with while traveling through Mexico the past couple years.

In the back were half-naked Burlesque dancers who'd been flown in from L.A. They were girls who were in love with this odd, unique craft that was from a bygone era. I could relate to that and appreciated their love for burlesque. The girls were not like your typical strippers who had hard bodies, six pack abs, or plastic surgery. They had a natural look with real curves and blemishes. They looked like women I would see in pictures from the 60's or 70's or movies set in those decades. They were like a Vegas dancer from the Rat Pack days.

The back was full of luchadores from Mexico, some big names and some mid carders. The big name on the poster was Blue Demon Jr. Blue Demon's father was one of the "Big Three" of lucha libre along with Mil Mascaras and El Santo. His father had been in multiple movies with Santo and was a big draw himself though he stayed in the shadow of Santo for his whole career. There were always stories of Blue Demon Sr being resentful of Santo's status in Mexico. Demon was a great wrestler who was charismatic in his own right, but he just wasn't the cultural icon Santo was.

The most interesting story I'd ever heard about Blue Demon Sr. was about a movie in which Mil Mascaras and he starred in together. They were battling their assortment of evil witches, zombies, or martians, I can't remember. But at the very end of the movie, El Santo appears to save the day with a special sci fi gun that thwarts the bad guys. Blue Demon was upset and resented Santo until his passing showing up at the end of the movie to steal his thunder!

Blue Demon Jr. was very gracious that night and took pictures with all us guys in the back and especially the girls. The other top guy in the back that night was Psycosis. Psycosis was Rey Mysterio's top rival for years in Mexico. He was a taller, Mexican guy who broke in about the time Rey did. They just clicked and had that special chemistry some guys have that a smart promoter is able to pick up and exploit. Psycosis was a great base for Rey to do all his high flying innovative moves and was unselfish working with Rey.

Psycosis was rewarded by going along internationally for the rise of Rey's star. The very first time I ever saw a tape of this amazing guy, Rey Mysterio Jr., everyone had been talking about was a WAR card in Japan. They did moves I'd never imagined let alone tried. Next, they tore the house down in Philadelphia for Paul Heyman's ECW where they really were introduced to an

American audience. When they signed both Rey and Psycosis in WCW during the Monday Night Wars, they could count on Psycosis to get Rey over. They would then have fantastic matches with every cruiser weight, Japanese, American, or Mexican they had.

On this night though, he was working without his mask. He had just signed with WWE and the word was he was going to be debuting for them in the coming months. He was just finishing up his dates he'd booked in the meantime.

The one thing I noticed right away was he sure looked jacked up. He was far more muscular and larger than I remembered him being on TV although he did wear a bodysuit when he wrestled back then.

I walked out to an area where the wrestlers made our entrances and watched his match. He seemed to be in a foul mood, but I'd never seen him work in person. So, I gave him the benefit of the doubt.

There was security at the Congress Theater that night that was largely made up of some bouncers. Some were larger than the boys, some not. The head bouncer was a Hispanic guy who was well over six feet tall and was also a big boy. He was in his twenties, very friendly, smiling, and was talking to all the boys while being professional.

Psycosis was well into his match that had spilled outside and was being aggressive with the fans and the bouncers. He just seemed pissed, in a foul mood, arrogant, and I thought was pushing the limits.

One thing led to another and one of the fans got a little too close to him. He got pissed and shoved the fan. I thought it was unnecessary, but I was giving him some leeway. Then Psycosis got in the head bouncer's face for letting the fan get so close and was really talking some shit. The bouncer was doing his best to diffuse Psycosis, but man I thought Psycosis was picking the wrong guy in the building to start shit with. I've never considered myself a tough guy, but I've always been observant of bad situations and this was starting to look bad. I thought it might end badly for Psycosis. This guy was a bouncer in an old theater that was in a rough part of Chicago. The bouncer was a big boy. He looked like he could kick some ass. Now I've met plenty of wrestlers who I'd put money on over this bouncer, but Psycosis didn't strike me as one of those tough guys.

Finally, Psycosis pushed the bouncer and that was the end of the bouncer's patience and friendly demeanor. He went after Psycosis. Amazingly, Psycosis seemed shocked by the bouncer's reaction and seemed genuinely surprised that he was being taken up on his aggression. I guess he was already feeling like a star and no one told this bouncer that.

Immediately, security began to scramble to get between the two and just at that moment I realized I was in my t-shirt, shorts, and sandals with my back against a wall. There was nowhere for me to go. If this situation got bad and we had several people fighting, I didn't have a place to go. If things got rough and I had to fight my way out, I wasn't in the best attire. On top of that I was in Chicago, not small town Iowa. So much for being observant.

Thankfully, the bouncer got cooled off right away. Like I said, he was a very friendly, professional guy. He probably realized that he might lose his job if he knocked out one of the main event wrestlers in the middle of his match. I couldn't blame him for standing up for himself though. He had every right to go after Psycosis.

We'll never know for sure, but I think that if Psycosis and the bouncer had gone at it that night the business would have lost. I'd always heard about Bill Watts having a rule in his territory that if you lost a fight in a bar or anywhere in public to a civilian you were fired. Watts said that wasn't exactly it. Watts had said, "If you were going to be in bars at night getting into fights, drinking, and causing problems, the business better win. If you weren't a tough guy, then don't be starting fights in bars. One guy did that, a top hand. He lost a fight and I looked at his hand and he didn't have any scars. I told him, 'You were a catcher last night, you didn't throw any punches' You're fired."

I wasn't a tough guy, so I didn't start fights. I thought Psycosis put himself in a bad, unnecessary position that night.

At the end of the end, I dropped off one of the older luchadores in Aurora and enjoyed hearing his stories of Antonio Pena, the booker of AAA wrestling, as well as the history of Mexican wrestling on TV.

It was a great, fun night. It was the kind of night and adventure I wanted all shows to be like. Because shows like Lucha Va Voom were so rare is probably why I appreciated that night so much.

CHAPTER THIRTY-SEVEN

Lesson From Seth Rollins

I continued all of 2005 working IPW shows, the Lucha shows, and a few more promotions here and there. We promoted another hometown show with Mr. Destiny and I headlined the card in a rubber match. We had some good Midwest talent like Egotistico Fantastico round out the IPW crew that made up most of the card.

As 2006 showed up, I maintained my schedule of IPW shows in Delta and did a few other shows for the Ritter brothers in my hometown. These were always fun shows, because their crew exposed me to some other talent in the Midwest. They paid me well and I always sold some merchandise, so it was a good payday with absolutely no expenses.

The highlight of the shows was personally witnessing the rise of Tyler Black, Colby Lopez, on the Indy scene. Tyler was still so young, in his late teens, but really was mature in how he approached the business. He was level headed and came across as humble with a quiet confidence.

The young girls loved him as he was a "white meat babyface." He had a great look with his gear and long hair. He kept himself in shape, was athletic, and enjoyed training. He could flat out wrestle, all his chain wrestling was smooth, and he was as natural a high flyer as I had ever seen. Being good looking and well over six foot I thought of what Jim Cornette said of a young Magnum T.A., "He was a puppy with big paws." He had the talent and genetics to grow into a star. He would only naturally gain more muscle and size as he got older.

Colby and his friend Marek Brave had been traveling around the Midwest and the country trying to make a name for themselves. They were both developing into talented independent wrestlers who promoters from different parts of the country wanted to book.

On one of the shows the Ritter's ran, Colby was getting an opportunity to wrestle the current TNA champion the "Phenomenal" A.J. Styles. Styles lived up to his name as he was and still is a phenomenal talent in the ring.

Colby was well aware of the opportunity the Ritter brothers were giving him and was prepared as always. I don't know for sure, but I think the Ritters felt Colby had earned this chance and were just trying to help him. They also were giving their anniversary card some star power as well.

The then Tyler Black pre ROH was calm and collected before the match. He didn't seem nervous yet was taking the match seriously. He obviously could handle pressure at this young age which was good. I remember seeing Tough Enough, the reality TV show M.T.V. and the WWE produced, when Al Snow, the head trainer, told a student who was complaining about the pressure to buck up. He said, "The pressure is only going to get bigger."

Sure enough Tyler Black and A.J. Styles had a great main event match that included some chain wrestling, some high spots, and told a great story. It was a basic, simple story that anyone could follow. The story of a young upstart who has a big future versus the current champion who is in his prime.

The match ended when A.J. hit his finish the Styles Clash. After the bout A.J. got on the mic and said he had just wrestled against the most impressive young guy he'd ever been in the ring with. He followed his words up by getting Tyler Black a match on TNA. Not surprisingly, TNA didn't follow up that match with anything. However, that didn't stop Tyler Black from making ROH his next stop and development into becoming a world-class wrestler.

Colby was eager to get trained even when he was a backyard wrestler and was already pretty damn good along with his friend Marek Brave. Then he was out working as much as possible in the Midwest. When I met him, he was still in high school and he told me his goal was to be in ROH. As soon as he made a name for himself in the Midwest, he pushed to improve and get matches against top talent like A.J. Styles. He traveled to Florida and worked dates there where the ROH booker Gabe Sapolski was impressed by him and he got to ROH.

There he kept improving, kept striving until he became a main event singles guy. Then he became their champion. Troy used Colby a few times on his IPW shows when it made sense like the big Hall of Fame show in Waterloo, Iowa, and a few fair shows in the summer. I booked him every chance I could for the shows I ran with Troy. It was a good chance for some of our guys like A.J.Smooth, Matty Starr, and Marshall Scott to work with a guy who had some different and broader experiences than they did. I always thought Colby was great to put on the poster. He was professional and gave you a great match on your card. We sold Polaroid pictures with fans in the ring with him, so it didn't cost a lot to use him as we made some of our money back.

The show in Columbus Junction didn't draw very well since it was a matinee show on a Sunday. But he really impressed me by watching every single match on the card and offering feedback and help to anyone who asked.

Looking back, there were a few things he was doing that I just rarely saw on our Midwest Indy scene. He was always in shape. He never showed up looking like he'd been slacking in the gym. Most guys didn't train. The ones that did train like me would sometimes slack off and only be in shape say nine months out of the year. You never know when your opportunity is going to come, so you should always be ready. Most guys have the attitude, and I was guilty of this, that you'll do the work if someone gives you the spot. Well, that's not how life works as I've learned.

He never took time off unless he was injured. As you've read in this book, that was my worst offense and one many guys commit. You take a "break." There are many reasons you take a break. You're having relationship issues. You say things like, "I'm burned out on wrestling!" You go back to school. Consistency is such a key to success, because success takes time. Usually, success takes far more time than you ever thought it would.

Colby had his first match in 2003 I think. He got called to the main roster of WWE in 2012. There were a lot of people that saw him being a guy who could make it to the roster. He did so many things right and it still took him nine years of consistent, hard work.

He was always improving. Colby was always taking that next step. So many guys have some set goals when they start. But once we reach a few of those goals, we lose steam or get complacent.

When I booked him for the couple shows Troy Peterson and I were running in Muscatine and Columbus Junction, I asked for some pictures for the posters and he told me to use any of the ones he had on his My Space page. On the page I was floored to read his goal in wrestling - Headline Wrestlemania!

Here was a kid who at that point just started in ROH and was publicly stating that was his goal. I had read a chapter in a Donald Trump book that was called "Think Big." The whole chapter was about how too many people dream small. When those dreams are small, they're not very exciting. Sometimes it's hard to put the work into something that just doesn't make your blood pump. It's hard to get excited about driving somewhere for a small payday and wrestling in front of a small crowd if you don't have that big dream to chase. If you don't see it as part of the journey that is going to get you to those exciting, big goals.

Also, too often we shortchange ourselves by not thinking big. I did that and saw a lot of my wrestling friends do that when our goal was to have a dark match in WWE or maybe even get signed by WWE. I've learned since then if you don't think big your mind doesn't go to work and get creative.

Patience was the last big lesson in life I observed from Colby's journey. I saw his consistent hard work. I watched his grit in grinding out all those drives, all those Indy shots in small crowds to learn his craft. I saw his time in the gym and clean eating. I knew of his over two year long stint in developmental in Florida before being called up to the roster. He was patient and knew Rome isn't built in a day no matter how tall, talented, good looking and athletic you are. It still takes time.

Colby may never know it, but I really learned a lot about what it takes to chase a big, elusive dream by watching his journey from the sidelines. I was able to tie concepts like "Think Big" and "Momentum" and other lessons from self help books to a real person's journey to the top. I've used the lessons and applied them to my real estate business and current wrestling career and I'm confident I will be more successful in those endeavors than I was in my early wrestling because of it. And Colby's still not done. I believe he will main event Wrestlemania!

CHAPTER THIRTY-EIGHT

Real Estate

In 2006 on the Monday after the Styles vs Tyler Black match I closed, I was aware the demands on my time were going to grow when I bought a fourplex in the nearby, small town of Grandview, Iowa. I also knew my gym time would suffer.

I got the idea to finally make the plunge and buy my first property after reading numerous books on investing, especially the book *Rich Dad Poor Dad* by Robert Kiosaki. But the big moment when I decided I would do it was when I was reading a biography of my bodybuilding hero Arnold Schwarzenegger. I had always read Arnold was a big-time real estate investor, but I had always assumed he started after he had been a movie star with big money to invest.

However, I was impressed and inspired when the biography documented Arnold lived a frugal lifestyle and saved his modest bodybuilding earnings. When he approached his mentor Joe Weider about where to invest his money, Weider suggested real estate because it would allow him the chance to continue his training while putting his money to work. He wouldn't have to monitor stocks daily, and Weider felt real estate was inherently less risky.

When I read that Arnold bought a modest 8-plex apartment and lived in one of the units himself, I thought, "That's what I'll do!" I had come to the point in life when I realized I didn't need a three bedroom house with a full basement when I lived alone. I was interested in investing, but I needed to reduce my expenses. I was already maxing out my 401k at work contributing twenty-five percent of my gross pay. I thought I could do what Arnold did and have my tenants make my house payment thus reducing my $900 I was paying monthly for my house.

After missing out on a few deals, I found an apartment I had lived in before, a fourplex with my brother Jorge back in 1998. I cut back some of my focus on wrestling. But, once I got used to being the landlord and manging my time accordingly, I kept working Delta and hitting the gym.

I began to wonder at this time if I would ever meet someone and get the chance to have a family. My buddy Troy Peterson had met a great girl and soon after she became Caroline Peterson.

My good friends were all married or had kids and I was getting to that age where if I didn't start soon I may not have any.   Dad was thirty-nine years old when my sister Isabelle was born, his last child. I always thought it wasn't when your dad had his first kid but when he had his last as the measuring stick of your time line. Well, I was getting close at thirty-three with no prospects in sight.

Then on New Year's Eve 2006 my brother Jorge and buddy Scott Canady invited me to go out to the bars. I wasn't too excited as I was tired of the bar scene. I was getting too old for it and hadn't found anyone at the bars whom I'd been able to have a serious relationship with. But as the night approached I agreed simply because I didn't want to spend it at the Casino as I had the year before.

Thank God I agreed. That night I met Tia Hall. We met since she had been drug out by our mutual friend Heather Monroe. Heather's brother Kevin Monroe was a good friend of my brother Ismael, because they played baseball together.

It was a fun night and Tia and I talked for a while. Later in the night Heather and Tia showed up at the restaurant we were at. We exchanged numbers, and I invited her to my company's upcoming Christmas party. Before she left we kissed.

I didn't get my hopes up as we went out on a date and began to talk on the phone. I still had been talking with Liliana in Mexico. I had been in so many casual relationships over the past couple of years where either me, or the girl, or both of us weren't interested in getting serious that I frankly expected the same.

But early in January before my company's holiday party, my siblings and I threw a fortieth anniversary party for my parents. I didn't invite a date, because I didn't want to bring a casual date to such an important night. My parents got to see many old friends from over the years and we had a very memorable night.

The highlight was after many hours of tacos, rice and beans, music, and Tequila   when Dad got on the microphone and gave a memorable toast and speech. He thanked everyone for sharing in the night. As the D.J. quietly played the song "Estabas Tan Linda" from my parents' favorite singer Marco Antonio Solis in the background without the lyrics, Dad finished his toast. Everyone in the room gave him a standing ovation. Then all the couples in the room, even the ones who I knew weren't in the happiest marriages, walked out to the floor and danced close together to the classic Mexican ballad. My dad's words, the night, and the music made even the most cynical couples romantic.

I, of course, stood alone in the back. I wasn't sad. I was actually very happy that we as a family made it a point to celebrate this great milestone and that my siblings and I still had my parents. But there was no doubt I was missing something. The New Year's before when Dad had made a wish for the New Year during a Mexican tradition he told me he wished for a wife for me. "A man isn't meant to be alone," he told me.

As I went home to the apartment that night, I parked my truck in the gravel lot in front of my unit, Apartment B. I lit up my Cuban cigar I had bought in Mexico and snuck through customs. As I took long drags off the Cuban Mohibo alone in the truck, still a bit numb from the tequila, I quietly said a prayer. I was tired of trying to pick my partner. It was in His hands. Whoever He told me to choose I would choose, I would trust His judgment.

CHAPTER THIRTY-NINE

Marriage

As Tia and I began to spend more time together in 2007, the other women who I'd left hanging in my mind drifted off and out of my life. They didn't want me and I didn't want them. We were just passing the time until something better came along.

Finally, something better came along for me. The eight years I'd lived alone and pretty much not in any real serious relationship taught me a lot about myself. I knew I wasn't the easiest person to live with always. I had some self-awareness and had seen that all relationships take work and aren't always all fun.

I still wasn't certain where Tia and I were going. We would meet at the Y after work to exercise together. We were spending time together and I was making some changes in how I approached fresh starts with her. I didn't do that dumb stuff single people do of seeing different people at the same time. I'd been there, done that, and it just didn't work for me. I didn't like it when it was done to me and it wasn't fair when I did it to someone else either. It sounds okay on paper, but it never worked emotionally for me any of the time I was single.

Tia went with me to a wrestling show for IPW and met Troy and Caroline Peterson. She didn't run away after seeing the world of Indy wrestling. On a dinner date at the local Chinese restaurant Peking, I told her I was finishing up wrestling soon and wasn't expecting to do it much longer.

Then Tia told me she was feeling different. She felt odd in the morning and with her stomach. We talked about it and agreed she should go to a doctor to find out if she was pregnant. She seemed nervous when she asked me how I would react if she was pregnant. I told her I was a grown man, we were in a relationship, and she was not a kid either. I had a great job that could support a family. I was very calm about it even if I can't explain why other than that night smoking my Cuban.

I'd also met her parents and they were good people who had been married for decades. I'd seen a few women who came from some messed up families when I was single and Tia came from a good background. It sounds crazy, but being thirty-three on the dating scene you met some crazy women. Some had addiction issues, some were distant and cold women who had daddy issues, some had crazy howl at the moon kids & exes. I'd seen it all, and Tia didn't have any of that.

She knocked on my door in Grandview after her doctor appointment with a card. I opened the card and it read that we were having a baby! I gave her a long hug and told her I was happy to hear the news. Again I felt calm and very good about the news. The next day or so I went downtown and bought a ring. We went to The Charthouse, a favorite restaurant spot next to the Mississippi, where locals park their boats and grab an unbreaded tenderloin and a beer. After dinner we walked to the rope swing by the dock, I got down on my knee and proposed. We were getting married, I was in love, and I was going to be a dad. Life was good.

Tia and I got married on July 20th of 2007 in a nice ceremony here in Muscatine. I knew wrestling wasn't my biggest priority when I told Troy Peterson I couldn't make a fair show that night because I was getting married. But I did find time to close on a house I planned on flipping that morning. Something Tia still occasionally gives me a hard time about!

As we were expecting our first baby, IPW and I promoted a few shows I wrestled on. But after the Fall, I didn't take any more bookings since we decided to move into the house in Muscatine I had planned on flipping. The housing market and the whole economy was showing signs of imploding and I couldn't sell the house at a price I was happy with. I was okay with that, because I thought we'd be better in Muscatine close to our parents when we needed help.

Tia called as my rapidly fat self was eating a huge two hamburger meal at my old employer of south end Hardess before I went in to work for a three-to-eleven shift. She told me she thought her water just broke. I called work and told Dean what happened and that I wouldn't be in. Dean, a proud dad who'd been through this many times, answered the phone and said, "Don't worry about work, Juan! Get to the hospital and good luck!"

After a long night in the delivery room, my daughter was born on January 20th 2008! We named her Arabella and she was a healthy, beautiful girl. The look she gave me with those big brown eyes when the doctor first handed her to me is a moment I'll keep with me forever. There is nothing like it.

Soon after I bought another rental house as the market continued to be slow. It looked like the economy was going into a deep recession and real estate was collapsing. Locally a major, good-paying employer went on strike. The strike drug on and many hard-working guys with families who were used to making great money were struggling. Another major employer, the largest employer in town, laid off workers and cut all overtime. Workers there went from working ten to twenty hours of overtime to losing jobs at worse. At best they were lucky to keep their forty hours. For the first time in my memory, things were getting scary.

I was fortunate that my employer had slowed down but not that bad and our jobs seemed secure. With that confidence, Tia and I bought a home for our family in a great neighborhood. We decided to rent the house we were living in. I decided with the baby, the uncertainty in the economy, and not exactly knowing how all these changes in life were going to affect my free time I wasn't going to buy anymore real estate for 2008.

I got a crazy idea though when I came back from a company meeting that had some great speakers. I was fat. I was thirty-five. I just got married and had a baby at home. But I was going to send my stuff to the WWE.

CHAPTER FORTY

Last Chance

When the great Eddy Guerrero died suddenly in November of 2006, many of us were shocked and saddened. Eddy came from the great Guerrero family and I had always been a fan of his. Hector of course had worked that Indy show for me in West Liberty years back. I felt terrible for his wife and kids. I felt terrible for the Latino wrestling fans also. Eddy was the biggest Hispanic star we had ever seen on a national scale. He was also the greatest wrestler of the Guerrero family and man that is saying something.

When Eddy died I think Vince McMahon and the wrestling community in general began to notice how fortunate wrestling was to have Rey Mysterio and Eddy. They were bilingual, great wrestlers and had an appeal to all nationalities. But I think McMahon had always been aware of how key the Hispanic audience was to wrestling. Dave Meltzer has written that statistically Hispanics are twice as likely to be fans than non Hispanics. Wrestling is a part of our culture and one we aren't embarrassed about. It has such a strong tradition in Mexico and with the growing Hispanic demographic in the U.S. it's critical that any wrestling company has good Hispanic talent on their roster.

A couple months after Eddy's death, people looked around and began to realize there just wasn't much talent being developed on the Indy's that was Latino. It slowly began to dawn on me as I read Dave Meltzer's *Wrestling Observer* that WWE was looking for new Hispanic talent. They were looking aggressively.

I knew I had a million strikes against me. I was over thirty, their usual cut off for signing the majority of new talent. I was at five foot nine inches not their ideal. I hadn't had a stellar ring career. I hadn't been to Japan, ROH, or Puerto Rico. They also had been pushing lately for athletes. They preferred division one level or even professional.

But I felt I had absolutely nothing to lose by trying. I had kicked myself when I watched the match of me and Chuck Palumbo vs The Barbarian and Griz in 2000 after Belly was born. I was good. I wasn't amazing, but I was good. I was a good enough athlete. Even though I wasn't six foot tall, the height of the average WWE wrestler had been going down. Stars like Guerrero, Rey, and others were changing the business. I knew I could get in shape and, as far as my age, I was never going to be any younger.

I had one giant thing going for me. I was a Mexican American who could speak both languages. My wrestling was good enough to get signed if I could get my look up to speed. I was different and I had something they needed that was in short supply.

I told Tia about my plans and she gave me the green light as well as her support. I called up Troy Peterson and told him my plans. He and I talked for several hours and he gave me some encouragement and advice on how to get my resume and pictures in front of the right person. It wasn't going to be easy, but I was going to hit the gym.

The first thing I did was put all my focus on getting in the gym. I simply thought of all the things I knew I needed to do to get as big and muscular as I could. Then I began to do them.

I took creatine on a daily basis. I took a pre-workout energy drink before every session. I bought an iPod and always trained with music. I ate a minimum of one gram of protein for every pound I weighed. I was consuming 220 grams of protein daily over four meals. I trained five days a week, stayed consistent, and did all the basic fundamental exercises that I knew worked. Bent over barbell rows, dips, bench press, military press, squats. I trained with intensity and focus, always trying to add weight when I could.

It took longer than I expected, about nine months, but it worked. My body got as big and massive as ever. I couldn't seem to get the muscularity I did in my late 20's, but other than that I felt good about how I looked.

CHAPTER FORTY-ONE
Thanking Skandar

Now came the hard part. Trying to get my resume in front of the right person. The WWE had really grown into a large international public traded company. When I was starting to work dates for Troy in Delta around 2003 or so, I remembered Gage Octane telling me he had talked a few times over the phone with Simon Dean when he was working for Jim Ross in talent relations. Tommy Dreamer was also working for J.R. during that time and Gage as well as Mr. Destiny Jay Hannah had both talked to those guys.

They were pretty accessible as talent relations was starting to realize the territories were dead. The guys that flooded the market from WCW when it closed down in 2001 had largely had their run and gone away or left the business. When I heard an online interview Simon Dean had done, they talked to him about his time as a talent scout. "I sat in the office and got tapes from all over the Indy's." The interviewer asked him how many of those tapes he saw. He responded, "Every single one of them. Let me tell you, I saw some terrible wrestling those years. Most of it was bad." But he did see every single tape he ever got. If I'd sent one in, it would have been seen. I would have got at least a phone call with some feedback.

Jay Hannah for years never sent anything in despite being trained by Brad Rehings, being over six foot, and having a great look. As soon as he sent his first tape in, he didn't hear anything. So, he called the offices and Tommy Dreamer answered. Jay asked if he'd seen his tape and Dreamer said no. He looked around his office and got back on the phone and said, "I got it here.   Whoa, big guy. Let me watch it and I'll call ya back." Fifteen minutes later Dreamer called him and set up a chance for Jay to get a look.

The real missed opportunity in my career was not seeing Mr. Akbar more. I would talk to Skandar on the phone a couple of times a year but not for any real long conversations. Ak was always better to talk to in person when it came to me. Every year I would drive through Dallas on my way to Eagle Pass or Mexico for vacations. I should have been stopping every single year to have lunch and say hi. Just to keep in touch, get advice, and offer any help. Building relationships is important, but maintaining them is even more critical.

It was around this time that Jim Ross had stepped down from talent relations and was replaced by Johnny Ace, aka John Laurinatius. Jim Ross ran a great division where he or the people working for him followed up on every inquiry or tape from a perspective talent. I didn't realize until 2008 just how far back Skandar Akbar and Jim Ross went. Skandar and Danny Hodge drove with a young Jim Ross in the Mid-South territory and helped educate him on the business. It was too late, but I now knew that if Skandar Akbar were to call Jim Ross he would get his call returned. But I never asked Ak for help, because I didn't feel I was good enough to even get a look in WWE when I was in my early 30's and finally working more and improving.

I decided to remedy a few of my young man mistakes. I thought about my network of people I knew who I could ask for help. With my resume I thought of Matt Murphy. Matt had applied for a writers job he told me when I saw him unexpectedly in Waterloo, Iowa, for a Harley Race show. I had gotten his contact info., so I got a hold of him. With Matt's help and suggestions, I put together a resume with some pictures that looked great.

Tia and I had planned a trip to Mazatlan with Belly in the Fall. I decided to drive down to Dallas a bit early while she flew to San Antonio to meet me and my parents there. I called Mr. Akbar and set up a time to meet lunch. I had no agenda other than to finally thank him in person for his training and to catch up.

When I drove to Dallas, I got a bit lost and had to ask Mr. Akbar for directions to the IHOP we were meeting at in Garland, Texas, where he lived. He knew that town so well. He asked me to look around and tell him what I saw. I described a couple buildings I saw and an exit. He said right away, "O.k., Juan, I know exactly where you are. Keep going on that road until you reach Jupiter exit…" Skandar directed me to exactly where I needed to be, always a road warrior.

When we met in the parking lot, we spotted each other right

away. As we shook hands, Mr. Akbar just kept grabbing my arms and shoulders saying how great I looked. "Man, Juan, you look in great shape! Look at you!" Ak was such an old gym rat, he understood the time and work it took to build a decent physique. It reminded me of when we first met and he beamed to his cousin Doug at the gym, "Look at them legs!" I had to admit I was happy to hear him express pride in me.

As the lunch progressed, it felt so good to catch up with him. He talked about some things we never got to before since the business was more open now and our relationship was in a different place. He talked about working in Tennessee when when he was young and how it was "the blind leading the blind." We talked about his run in the WWE where he was supposed to get a shot against the great Bruno Sammartino.

We also touched on a sensitive subject, his marriages. He actually brought up my ex-wife.

He asked, "What was her name Juan?"

"Sarah", I answered.

He smiled, "I liked her. She was sweet. She was a funny girl."

When I mentioned Peggy, his wife at the time I was training, he said they had divorced amicably a few years back. He lived alone and seemed content with it.

I asked him how his wife previous to Peggy handled the era of the 70's when he was gone for long stretches of time. "I tried to really take care of her when I was here. Do everything I could for her. She was understanding, but I didn't want to push it."

His wife during that era passed away young. She seemed to be the love of his life. She must have been very understanding as he spent time away for long stretches in New York for Vince McMahon Sr. as well as a long stint in Australia. For a period of time, he booked Mid-South and was also a talent there and it was known as a hard driving territory. But he lived the life he wanted to live and loved the business deeply. He wouldn't have wanted it any other way.

As we finished up lunch, I mentioned I was trying to get a dark match in WWE. He said he knew Johnny Ace and would try to put a call in. I told him I appreciated it. I knew Ak had gotten

Slam Shady, one of his students after me, several dark matches in the early 2000's. But that was the Jim Ross era. He did know Johnny Ace as Ace had gotten his start in Mid-South/UWF as a flag bearer for The Sheepherders.

Regardless, the reason I wanted to come was to thank him for his training and all he had done. He shrugged it off but appreciated my visit. "You love it! Juan, you love the business and that's why you're still doing it. It's good to see you." We hugged outside and said goodbye.

Two years later Skandar Akbar died. I came home from the graveyard shift and checked my Facebook account. Steve Shettler, the ring announcer from Sigourney, Iowa, sent me a message. He asked me if I'd heard. There was an article from the Slam Canoe website saying Ak had passed away at the age of seventy-five. It affected me more deeply than I expected. As you get older, you appreciate those who helped you when there was little in it for them. Skandar Akbar was a sweet, generous man with a kind heart in a tough business. He had a soft spot for young wrestlers and helped far more than the few who became mega stars. But the biggest star in the history of the business Stone Cold Steve Austin will tell the story of sitting in the backseat driving to the next town while he got an education on the craft of wrestling form Skandar Akbar and Bronco Lubich in the front. Ak's legacy lives on.

CHAPTER FORTY-TWO

Too Little, Too Late

As 2008 went on and I felt in shape, I mailed my resume into Florida Championship Wrestling in Tampa, Florida, where WWE had their developmental school. I also sent one in to John Lauranitis and Mark Curano in Stamford, Connecticut. I knew it was going to be tough to get through the red tape of the office as I hadn't heard glowing words about how Lauranitis ran talent relations. He wasn't nearly as organized as the workaholic Jim Ross and his lieutenants who looked at tapes were not clearly defined. Secretaries kept Curano and Lauranitis tightly screened.

Looking back, I should have heeded Troy Peterson's suggestion to attend Harley Race's tryout camp he was putting together in the fall. Ricky Steamboat would be there and the seminar would have done me some good as well. But I thought I'd try to get a look first through these channels. I didn't have time on my side, so I don't know what I was thinking.

As the Winter of 2008 set in and we came into 2009, it was obvious I wasn't getting anywhere. I received exactly zero phone calls or responses to my calls, e mails, and resumes. One morning after a long, cold graveyard, I tried to stay up to make a call to Harley Race. I was hoping he might have something, anything for a suggestion on finding out if my resume had even been looked at. Maybe it'd been looked at and I sucked. I could handle that, I just wanted some feedback. Exhausted, I called at 9 AM but just got the answering machine. I was turning thirty-six soon and I began to realize the WWE ship may have sailed.

I should have been doing this at thirty or sooner. Not at this age. I woke up the next day and slowly gave up hope anything would happen with my resume. Time would prove me right.

CHAPTER FORTY-THREE

Baby Boy

As I turned thirty-six, I let wrestling drift off my priority list. I worked a show for Troy in Wilton, Iowa, and it went well. Other than that, my focus turned to family and work. Tia and I decided to try to have another child. I also continued to look for more real estate opportunities as well as other businesses.

I read in the classified that a small coffee shop on my drive to work was for sale. It'd closed down under sudden circumstances and now was available. I thought it was a good deal and, after discussing it with Tia, we thought we could manage and operate it ourselves. Tia could open it in the morning and I'd run it on the weekends. The fact we were in the middle of a major recession didn't faze me. I had so much confidence in our recovery that we went forward and purchased it.

It was a disaster. I'd broken so many rules when I purchased the business. The biggest rule was entering an industry I didn't have any experience in. I thought my Hardees experience would help, and it did to an extent. However, operating a business is one thing, buying it is another. On the first day, I served customers myself. I realized we had a terrible location. Businesses serving espresso and lattes like Starbucks cater to high-end clients. They cater mainly to women and professionals.   Our location was very blue collar with few women.

We delivered a great product and Tia turned out to be a great barista. She was a quick learner thanks to the trainer we hired named Heather. The fact was that we were in a terrible stage in life with a toddler and trying to have another baby to learn to operate a small business. It lost money in the beginning, but we had signed a one-year lease. We were committed to ride it out and try to turn it around.

We did get good news when we found out Tia was pregnant with a boy in the summer! Tia had a challenging pregnancy in the fall and got kidney stones on Thanksgiving. She was hospitalized, but they weren't able to remove the stones until after our son was born. The pregnancy continued to be a struggle and we along with our doctor decided to induce Tia early. There are always risks when you decide that, but we didn't think Tia was going to be able to carry the baby full term.

On January 5th, Alex was born. He had a rough first night, but after that he was deemed healthy and doing well! He would be the first boy to carry on the family name. We agreed on the name Alex, because I always wanted my kids' names to have something that told the world they were Latino and everyone could easily pronounce. We both liked the name Alex and a lot of prominent Hispanics have the name such as Alex Rodriguez the ball player. In a small way, he also was named after "The Pug" Alex Porteau, my trainer!

Tia was scheduled to have another surgery soon after the delivery to remove the kidney stones. Before we knew it, we were trying to handle a newborn, medical bills, a failing small business, and Tia's health. Life was tough at that time. It really was the toughest period of my life as I knew I had to just keep moving forward. My job at the plant was my biggest asset. As I saw my 401k shrink along with the rest of the country, I wondered how I was going to dig out of this mess.

Life wasn't much fun at that time with our money problems. But after deciding to sell the coffee shop when our lease was up, we took a deep breath. I stepped on the scale and I was embarrassed to see I weighed 242 pounds with none of it muscle. I hadn't stepped in a gym for over six months. I turned thirty-seven in March of 2010, now it was May and I needed to do something.

CHAPTER FORTY-FOUR

Waterloo H.O.F.

We spent 2010 digging out of our financial hole and grateful we no longer had to run a business day to day. I managed to buy two properties in 2009 despite the struggle with money, credit, and time. I figured out how to buy one property in 2010, a foreclosure, with some creative financing. But after that I was froze out of any investments since I couldn't come up with the twenty percent cash down banks like to see. During the greatest sale on real estate in my lifetime, I had to sit out most of the year investing. The lessons just kept coming.

Still when I looked around town, I knew I was still in a better spot than most. I had my job, my house, and Tia's health was good again. I kept digging out during 2010 as I kept in touch with Troy Peterson with our talks and occasional visits to Des Moines. We did promote a couple shows together, where we featured a new Muscatine wrestler Micheal Rhodes. Micheal was a good-looking, tall, black wrestler who'd been training with Travis up in Algona. The shows drew decently and they served a purpose of getting me to hit the gym.

In 2011 I was beginning to wonder if maybe wrestling was done for me. I was getting older, and it was obvious there weren't any big opportunities for me at my age. However, Troy called me up in the spring with some big news. He and the George Tragos/Lou Thesz Wrestling Museum in Waterloo, Iowa, were organizing an exciting new event for the big Hall of Fame weekend in July. Gerald Briscoe and Jim Ross would be hosting a tryout for independent wrestlers. Troy asked if I'd be interested in helping out the afternoon of the tryout.

I jumped at the chance to be a small part of the event. It was a big deal for these two WWE Hall of Famers to come to Iowa. It also showed the fact Troy was growing as a promoter and organizer in the wrestling community. It was a great opportunity for all Midwest Indy wrestlers and a chance for Troy's IPW promotion to be spotlighted on the Friday evening show. I thought it would be a learning experience for me, even if it was too late for it to benefit my in ring wrestling career.

The afternoon was a new experience for all involved as this was the first time Jim Ross and Gerald Briscoe had been able to panel a tryout together. The opportunity to see over thirty Indy wrestlers in six minute matches live was valuable for them. It gave them the chance to see things you can't see on a DVD. The chance to see that many bodies in one afternoon was valuable for their time as well. Also, the museum benefited because the entry fee paid by the wrestlers all went to the museum. The wrestlers benefited greatly for the chance to get great feedback from two of the greatest minds in wrestling who had over seventy years experience in a variety of talent and administrative capacities.

Gerald had been an agent for Vince McMahon since he retired from the ring in the mid-eighties. He was part of McMahon's inner circle and helped guide so much talent such as Steve Austin and The Rock. He was a talent agent at this time capable of signing a talent to a WWE contract.

Jim Ross had been V.P. of Talent Relations and helped build the best money drawing locker room in the history of wrestling during the Attitude Era of the WWE. He also had worked for two of the greatest minds in the history of wrestling, Bill Watts and Vince McMahon.

As the tryout started, Troy was kind enough to give me a choice spot. I was to sit next to Gerald and Jim and give them the pictures and resumes of the wrestlers involved in the match in front of them. I was to answer any questions they might have on the talent wrestling. It was a tremendous opportunity to be a fly on the wall while these two evaluated talent.

I felt for the young guys involved because they had nerves and pressure while I got to enjoy the event without any of that. The biggest sin the guys were committing was going too fast. I heard both Briscoe and Ross say, "These kids need to slow down." The guys had their nerves and the perceived pressure of the six minute time limit against them. To many of the young wrestlers six minutes seemed too short to show their talents off. But I was learning the opposite was true as the event unfolded. Within two minutes or less, Briscoe and Ross could tell if someone had any talent or skills to warrant further review.

The really great wrestlers who tried out, such as Colt Cabana, you could see their skills as soon as they locked up. His match was eye-opening. Everyone in the room could see the difference in skill level and experience. It was obvious. Now, it's not really fair to all that tried out to compare Cabana to them as he actually was a signed wrestler in the WWE who had been in their developmental system. He knew what the WWE liked and had actually been polished by them. But his match really highlighted the difference in his in ring performance.

After the tryout ended, Ross asked me if we had a room everyone could go to where Briscoe and he could talk to the boys. Troy got a room in the back closed off and the second part of the session began, perhaps the most valuable. Briscoe and Ross began to talk for about an hour on what they had seen the guys do right and what they had done wrong. It was gold. The information I heard from those two and then Terry Funk was priceless information for a young wrestler. They said one of the worst offenses they had seen that afternoon was far too common on the Indy scene. They said, "Everyone was trying to get their shit in." A tendency we Indy workers have is of getting our "moves" in, rather than making the match the focus.

After the session tryout was over, my mind was reeling from the experience. It did turn out to be a valuable experience for gaining knowledge. Those two guys taught me more in that afternoon of listening to them and sitting next to them than any match, any opponent ever did. It was worth years of experience on the Indy scene.

Yet, after the tryout I was surprised to hear some of the Indy wrestlers in denial. They were guilty of some of the mistakes pointed out about their appearance and work. One wrestler who is very talented but refuses to step foot in a gym told me nothing he heard in the room applied to him!

When the evening's wrestling card began, I was lucky enough to sit next to Austin Aries at his merchandise table. Aries had just been signed by TNA after a long and financially difficult struggle on the Indy scene. He didn't participate in the tryout as he was a signed wrestler, but he watched and heard the feedback session afterward. I was eager to hear his impressions on the afternoon.

Aries told me he didn't see anything that surprised him

unfortunately. He said, "Those guys trying out didn't understand something. There was not one move they could perform in front of those two guys that was going to impress them. And all they kept trying to do was moves."

The truth was I had to tip my hat to all the wrestlers who participated.   They put themselves out there to be criticized and that's not easy. They traveled from all over the country and paid hard-earned money. The easy path is to not put yourself in the arena and pretend you're still great. I'd been guilty of that over the years. I'd never had such a great opportunity like this so close, but I had the Japan tryout happen with Harley Race and I passed like a coward. A few of these guys who've tried out I've seen come back the next year better and improved with the knowledge they've gained from the previous year's tryout. That's far better than I ever did, so I commend those competitors.

CHAPTER FORTY-FIVE

Hacksaw

As the year progressed, I had to ask myself the question all wrestlers do. How much longer? I still felt good health wise. Since I never worked a crazy style and never worked full-time, I thought I had a lot of bumps left in me. But I also knew the window was closing. I wasn't going to be the best wrestler on the card regardless of what kind of shape I was in. The WWE and any major promotion wasn't going to happen. I simply wasn't good enough, and I was at an age I wasn't going to get to the in ring work skill needed.

Yet, there was no denying I still enjoyed wrestling. I enjoyed talking about it, reading about it, learning about it, and being around it. As 2012 rolled around, I asked Troy if he could put me on some shows. He, as always, was generous enough to book me.

These days there is talk in artists, singers and writers communities of returning to an age old business model. One of finding one or many patrons to support and fund your art, your craft. PayPal, YouTube and many other modern technologies make this possible these days.

The first time I ever heard that concept I realized Tory Peterson had been my patron. The patron of my art, my craft.

I did a well attended fundraiser in nearby Maquoketa, Iowa. I still weighed in heavy, around 232 pounds and was not the most consistent in the weight room. I was put in the opening match against a young, good-sized, athletic wrestler Nate Ailsun. We had a good match and I got plenty of heat. I had a lot of fun as we started the show off strong and did our job. It was great that both my kids were able to see their daddy wrestle, though

Arabella cried the instant ref Billy Jay counted to three and I lost.

A few months later, I wrestled A.J. Smooth. A.J. had spent the past couple of years developing into a great hand in the ring. He had improved his look as well and was a guy I wanted on every card I booked. In the back A.J. and I put together a match blueprint and, frankly, I was fine letting him lead me to a good match. He was the sharper pro now and I was cool with it.

After those few bouts, I asked Troy to keep me in mind for his fair shows he runs in the summer. He books half a dozen or so. They are well attended, pay well, and are a lot of fun.

Troy once again took care of me and made me realize I simply wouldn't have an independent wrestling career if I had never met him. The shows for the summer of 2012 had a couple of added bonuses. One bonus was that most of the shows were going to be held in the same week, and they would all be near the Cedar Rapids area. Troy and most of the IPW crew was going to be staying at a centrally located hotel in Cedar Rapids and he got us a great rate. This would allow us to drive every night an hour or less one way to each night's show, go back to the hotel, and do it all over again the next night. We had a bar in the hotel, restaurants open late nearby, and a nice pool where Tia and I could spend time with the kids. We would be gypsies that week as a family.

The second bonus was WWE Hall Of Famer and wrestling legend "Hacksaw" Jim Duggan was booked on most of the cards as well. It's always fun and a learning experience to be in the same locker room as a veteran like Hacksaw.

First, we started with a fair show in Boone, Iowa, where I wrestled Danny Wagner. Danny was part of that great IPW training class put together years ago. We had a good solid match where I cut my usual anti-American promo. I felt bad for the Hispanic family who was in attendance when I got my response of U.S.A. chants. Also, the heat from the crowd was not quite as strong as it used to be. It seemed like times were changing. People were becoming more used to Latinos in their community and our culture. I also was changing as well after becoming a parent. I felt for that Hispanic dad who brought his little kids to enjoy some wrestling.

Danny and I worked again at the Hall of Fame show in Waterloo where Troy and I agreed it would be best for me to be a babyface. I cut a promo expressing my roots of Texas wrestling and thanking the Hispanics in the audience for their support in Spanish. The promo was well received. Danny and I had a short but good bout.

The Cedar Rapids gypsy week started off at a nicely attended fair show where I wrestled Mitch Stuefan. Mitch was the babyface and I was the heel as usual. Mitch and I had a good match and I felt in the best shape I'd been in a while. I had begun lifting seriously and consistently again. I wasn't as lean as I needed to be, but I looked like an athlete.

As Tia, the kids, and I enjoyed the week, the hotel, and the pool, Troy and Travis called me at the hotel one morning. Troy said, "Trav and I have been talking about tonight's Main Event. We kind of think the best person to have wrestle Hacksaw is you. Would you be up to that?"

I thought about it for a second and gave him the only answer I could, "Of course, I'd love to wrestle Duggan." I had been around long enough to agree with something I'd heard Troy tell many Indy wrestlers, "When people ask you about your wrestling, you're not going to bring up you and Travis or Matty having a great match that tore the house down in Delta. You're going to tell them about working a famous wrestler."

I knew that to be a fact, as over the years when I explained to people what independent wrestling was, it was always easier and more interesting to them to share stories of a famous wrestler you met over the years or had a chance to wrestle.

This was a great opportunity to learn something, a great chance to have fun, and have a great story to tell people now as well as years later. Plus, I had a chance to be in the Main Event, something I hadn't done nearly enough. The pressure would be good and the night memorable.

The night began by going to Maquoketa early to enjoy the parade held by the Jackson County Fair with my family. After the parade, Tia and I took the kids to the midway. There they got to enjoy some fun rides, and we got some memorable pictures of them both. The evening's weather was perfect and the mood at the well-attended fair was fantastic.

As Tia and the kids settled in at the merchandise table, I went to the trailer where Hacksaw and I would hang out while we waited for the Main Event. As soon as we sat down, I made it a point to soak this night in as much as possible. I was sharing a locker room with a man who was not only a WWE legend, but, even more important to me, a Mid-South icon who was a huge star in my favorite territory. He also spent a lot of time with my trainer Skandar Akbar.

Right away Hacksaw began with the stories and I just sat and listened. I asked him about the Von Erich family and, like so many veterans, he wanted to talk about Fritz. So many of the veterans like Skandar and Dusty Rhodes and others talked about Fritz as such a towering presence, a dominant influence in that area of the country. Duggan was no different.

"I got a lot of respect, a lot of love for Fritz. He met me when I was playing football in college. He talked to me about getting into the business after college. I kind of blew him off, I was going to play in the NFL I thought. Then after a few knee injuries and football ending, I called him up. He broke me in and I'll always have a special place for Fritz." Duggan stated.

It turned out Texas was an important place for Duggan as he started in the Sportatorium after some training. Eventually after a few territories where he was floundering, Bruiser Brody called him up to work in the San Antonio territory. Duggan always credits that time for being where he really began to "get" the business and develop a character.

We talked about the late Curt Henning and Duggan said something that echoed what Hector Guerrero had told me years earlier. He said, "Curt was a second generation guy. All those guys, DiBiase, the Guerreroes, all those guys, they get our business so much better than the rest of us. They have that something special."

He told a great story about the Hawaii territory which was notorious for being in paradise, but not paying well at all.

Duggan, like so many young wrestlers of that era, found himself there as it was a good place for green wrestlers to go to get some experience. He reminisced, "The crowd always had so many Samoans. And they love to fight. We had a riot there and hell I was young, just got out of the NFL and weighed 300 pounds all jacked up. I was ready to fight. I saw some giant Samoan coming after me and I put up my fists and said 'let's go!' I hit him with everything I had! He just shook my punch off and snorted! That's the last thing I remember. That was the only time ever, in the ring, in football, I've been knocked out cold!"

Duggan at this point was in his late 50's, but man he was still massive. He had paws that were enormous. His fists looked like they could destroy people. He was a natural athlete as he had been a state champion wrestler, had a great college football career, and had a spell as an Atlanta Falcon. He was a throwback to the wrestlers of yesterday. He was a big, tough guy who had a wild side. In his younger days, he was full of piss and vinegar! He loved to fight and did it well. The stories of him and Hercules Hernandez as well as "Dr. Death" Steve Williams clearing out bars in the Mid-South days were legendary. I believed every one of them.

Duggan was a character as well. There was no way he could have survived a corporate job and life. Like all the wrestlers of his generation, they were cut from a different cloth. The travel, the competition, the money, and the fast life of wrestling was home to them.

But Duggan was also one of the few of his generation who had his life in a good spot. He had a beautiful wife and two daughters at home. He'd saved his money and was still making good money on the Indy scene. He was also on a legends contract with WWE which kept some steady money coming in.

After a great night of listening to some classic stories, Duggan and I got ready to go out for the Main Event. I was proud that I was having Duggan's first singles match for IPW as Troy had booked him previously in tags and six man matches to make it easy for Hacksaw. As we headed out for the Main Event, Duggan smiled and turned to me. He said, "Hey, let's do it for old Skandar!"

Duggan and I had a good match that entertained the crowd, and I was glad my family was able to see it as well. Duggan was happy with the match and I felt good we got the job done. It was a memorable night and one all my friends and coworkers thought was cool. Duggan was one of those names so many people remember from the heyday of the WWE Hogan era.

We finished up the summer run with a few more shows that all went well. We made some money, the matches were good, the trips were short, and my family and I had fun.   It's the way you hope wrestling can always be.

CHAPTER FORTY-SIX
Luchador

Against Tony Sly for 3XW. Photo by Peyton Mitchell

After the fun summer run ended, I had a lot of time to reflect on wrestling. IPW didn't have any other shows planned nearby. They would run their weekly cards in Algona, Iowa. I was always welcome to be a part of those shows, but the drive was a solid four hours one way. After gas it left very little in the pocket, and the long drive necessitated I pretty much spend my weekend away from my family. I would arrive home early Sunday morning and sleep in until nine or ten A.M. If I worked the graveyard shift that week, it meant I went in to work Sunday night at 11 P.M. It left little time for my family.

Regardless, I couldn't get over how much I enjoyed that summer. Wrestling always gave me a reason to go to the gym when I might want to skip a day or two. If I knew I was wrestling, it also kept my diet and weight somewhat in check.

But I also knew some things had to change. As I had gotten older, the sports wrestlers in the ring got even younger. I had heard veteran Tom Prichard in an interview say wrestling was a "young man's sport." I didn't understand what he meant when I heard that. I mean he was still a fantastic wrestler, could work at a good clip, and was an asset to any card. Now, I was beginning to understand.

Even if you keep yourself in shape, you can't hide your age.

Your face shows your years. My hair was graying and my mustache was graying even faster. The thought of long drives to boring Midwest towns I had already been to didn't appeal to me anymore. Traveling away from my family for little money also didn't sound fun.

The guys involved in wrestling were getting younger and younger. When I started in Texas, it was rare to see anyone under twenty-one in the locker room. There were always a few guys over forty. Most of the roster was made up of wrestlers in their thirties and a few young guys in their twenties. Now, it was common to see a teenager or two. Almost all the rest of the talent was in their twenties. There would be maybe one or two guys in their early thirties. A forty year old was a rarity. And I would be turning forty the following March.

I also didn't like being a heel anymore, especially an anti-American heel. There were more and more Hispanics showing up at cards, and I always thought it was bad business to alienate or make your paying customers feel uncomfortable.

One other negative to being a heel was it affected your merchandise sales. I had been selling Mexican lucha libre masks for kids and adults for years. It was a great way to make a few extra dollars, sometimes a lot of dollars. I would buy the masks during my travels in Mexico or my parents would when they traveled back to Eagle Pass, Texas. But I could never be at my table selling my masks and I couldn't try to sell pictures or t-shirts like other successful Indy wrestlers. My job was to make people dislike me.

Tia had told me it would help us sell more masks if there was a masked wrestler on the card like there had been at one time. Super Cito Kid was an IPW wrestler who wrestled under a mask. Troy had helped him come up with his gimmick and he was a talented high flyer who appealed to kids. But he never pushed his merchandise and eventually left wrestling.

One day while in the shower that fall, I came up with an idea that had been brought up to me several times by others - become a masked Mexican luchador. I can't really say why I never embraced the idea before when Mario and a few others would throw it out. Maybe it was because I enjoyed being a heel at the time. Maybe it was because I never wanted to wrestle under a mask, I don't know. But at that moment in the shower when the picture of a Mexican luchador came into my mind, it grabbed me.

It solved all my problems. I could be a good guy again. Now that I'd been a heel for so long I knew much better what a good babyface is supposed to do. I already was a good enough wrestler to work pretty much eighty percent of all the places on the Indy scene.

I would be able to sell more merchandise. I could have a character that appealed to kids and Hispanics. It could be put on pictures, t-shirts, caps, and bandannas. The Lucha masks that already sold well could sell far better now. I could take Tia's suggestion and be that masked wrestler on the card.

The mask would cover my graying mustache and hair. Under a hood you become almost timeless as long as your work and body are still in good shape. I still felt, when I dedicated myself, I could have a physique better than most on the roster. I would never be the guy in the best muscular shape anymore, but I didn't need to be.

I no longer needed to feel guilty about alienating Hispanics in the audience. I could give them something to be proud of and cheer! This probably was the most appealing factor to me. The masked Mexican luchador is an icon around the globe. All over the world people recognize the Masked luchador as a symbol of Mexican culture. A positive symbol, a heroic one. Thanks to movies of the Mexican Cinema as well as legendary Latino wrestlers such as Mil Mascaras, Rey Mysterio, Sin Cara, and El Santo the Mexican luchador was known worldwide. The character wouldn't need to be explained to the audience.

I knew right away I wanted to be more of a classic luchador, a throwback to the 70's. Like Mil Mascaras and Blue Demon, I wanted to be colorful and heroic. As a wrestler, it is critical to be different and I would be unique to a promoter, something hard for them to replicate.

I read an interview with Steven Regal, a WWE wrestler who had been training wrestlers at the WWE developmental center in

Tampa. He said to think about who you really enjoyed watching as a child. Who caught your eye? Then study them. Too often as wrestlers we start as fans but once we begin to train and have matches we are drawn more and more to the wrestler who's technical skills are the best. That's o.k. in one sense, but you dismiss some of the biggest drawing, most popular performers of the industry.

I had heard so many wrestlers criticize and belittle the Ultimate Warrior and I would fall for that trap at times. But I was mesmerized when he described in a shoot interview how he developed the character. He talked about going into the fabric store in Dallas to get a few colorful pieces. He couldn't afford much, so he only purchased one color of face paint and one color of fabric. But he obsessed about his character, his gear, his interviews, and his physique. His "moves" in the ring were at the bottom of his priorities.

I looked at superheroes from the Marvell movies that had been making millions such as Thor as well as my favorite, a D.C. comic, Superman. I watched my son Alex. I saw what drew him in, what superheroes he liked. I thought about the Star Wars movies that I loved as a child as well as some of the campier guilty pleasures such as Flash Gordon. What did all these have in common?

It was obvious I would have to invest in some new gear, colorful gear. I had another advantage here. Unlike so many Indy wrestlers who were broke, I could afford to invest in some quality gear. I needed to be different than most Indy wrestlers, so I would go all out and get a quality mask that was unique and custom fitted for me. Not a Rey Mysterio or Mil Mascaras mask like I'd seen countless times on cards. I would buy a colorful cape and wristbands. I would paint my boots and bling them up!

The star I studied more than any other was Mil Mascaras. I knew my weakest selling point was going to be my work in the ring. I was good, but not great. Mascaras frankly never had many great matches. He was considered selfish in the ring and so his opponents never worked too hard to make the matches great. I looked at this as a positive. Both Mil and The Ultimate Warrior were not considered talented technicians like a Shawn Michaels but they were mega stars. So, it was obvious to me in ring skills were not the most important thing when it came to marketability.

What Mascaras did have was incredible gear. His masks, tights, and capes were beautiful, colorful, and updated constantly. He had a great physique for his era being a former Mr. Mexico bodybuilding competitor. He had that superhero look that I wanted.

I figured being able to speak Spanish would come in handy again as it would create an authenticity to my gimmick. I had lots of ideas, now it was time to put them together and see if it would work in real life.

CHAPTER FORTY-SEVEN

Developing The Character

Dropkicking Christian Rose for SCW. Photo: Matt Tucker

I spent the winter checking out sites to buy lucha gear online and in social media. I was able to find a talented Mexican mask maker living in Chicago, Chilanga Mask, to make my mask and tights. I ordered my boots and cape from Deportez Martinez in Mexico City.

I knew after my years in wrestling, as well as real estate and how things operated at the plant, to not wait for perfection on my gear. After studying ideas and gear makers, I had to order something and expect problems and mistakes. I would course correct as the gimmick evolved. What was important was starting.

Things went well at first as the dreaded Mexican standard time I had known in my culture didn't apply to Deportez Martinez. They gave me a four week time line and kept it. The boots were not a perfect fit, but they looked great with their shiny gold glitter look. My cape fit perfectly and stood out with its metallic gold base and silver lining. The shipping was a bit pricey out of Mexico City, but the price of their gear was low and helped compensate.

Chilanga Mask took longer than promised and ran on Mexican standard time. But after a delay and with my first booking with the character rapidly approaching, Luis got my gear to me the Thursday before the show. The color was not what I had ordered though. Rather than red and gold the gear was black and silver with red trim. The boots and cape would not match. But I had to hand it to Luis as the mask was a perfect fit and looked incredible as well as the tights.

Tia and Troy tried to get me to overlook my disappointment in the color mix-up. Tia thought the black actually looked masculine, tough, and made me look slimmer. Troy thought I should let Luis know about the mix-up and give him a chance to make it up to me. I had always had plans on buying multiple colors of gear to make me appear like a star, so black, silver, and red would be one of the color schemes! I bought some paint and, with some nerves, Tia and I painted my original and only boots I've ever owned red and used silver holograms for the letters. I feared ruining my boots I got all those years ago from a famous boot maker out of Arkansas. The boots had been in so many rings over the years and were priceless to me. To my relief, the boots looked pretty good after drying and I was ready to go with the new character!

After lots of thought, I decided to keep the name Latin Thunder. No matter what I came up with, I just couldn't compete with that fifteen-year-old Hispanic kid who dreamed up the name in homeroom class. I had discussed it with Troy, and he felt a Spanish name would be more authentic with a more exotic, international feel to it. While I understood where he came from as Mascaras was the "man of a thousand masks," I wanted something that whites could pronounce. I had noticed while thinking of the name that the majority of Japanese and Mexican stars had names that implied their ethnicity, but were easy to pronounce. Antonio Inoki, The Great Muta, Kabuki, Giant Baba, Blue Demon, Atlantis, and Blue Panther.

I wrestled my old friend Montoya X in a low-pressure match

for both of us. It was Juan's first day back after a long lay off, and I just wanted to debut the gimmick, find out what worked, and what needed improvements. I was nervous about how it would feel to wrestle with a mask on, something I'd never done. It was a warm, summer night and the mask completely covered my face with no openings for my nose or mouth. I wasn't claustrophobic, but I got a small feeling of that as I put the mask on.

The crowd was small at the fair show, which helped keep the pressure low for Juan and I. The match went well considering the circumstances. Juan did fine even if he got winded quickly. His timing was as good as ever and he never hurt me. I got a good reaction from the crowd and, though wrestling under the black mask in the heat was challenging, I did fine. The locker room loved the gear, and it felt good to finally get real feedback on this idea I'd been working on for over six months.

The next show with the character was the Lee County Fair where I wrestled a good, young wrestler Aaron Luft. Troy gave me good feedback afterward on my entrance. After entering the ring, I took my expensive, beautiful looking cape and wadded it up in a heap and handed it to someone at ringside. Troy said the cape looked expensive until I handled it so carelessly. He suggested I make a slow, careful display of taking off the cape and folding it gently before gingerly handing it to the ringside attendant who would also handle it carefully. It was great advice and showed the need to get feedback as you could never pick up every subtle movement you were making. Jake "The Snake" Roberts had said years ago his character started the moment his music hit and he walked to the ring. His pace, his eyes, and his entrance set the tone for his character. As Indy wrestlers we didn't always think of that initial impression we set long before the bell rings.

I knew we were creating something that stood out and had showmanship when the local paper featured a picture of our match in the story about the wrestling that night at the fair.

The big test that was tailor-made for my character was the Latino Festival held in Des Moines that had featured wrestling from 3XW, an Indy fed that was headed by Todd Countryman, Mad Dog McDowell, and a few others. I contacted Todd and expressed interest in working the show as I felt I could add a lot to the card. I was interested in the response my gimmick would get from the mix of festival goers who included a large amount of Hispanics. I thought I might get a picture in the Des Moines Register and, hopefully, make some contacts for personal appearances.

As the date arrived in early September, the heat was intense. Tia and I went with the kids and my in-laws Brenda and Mike Hall. Tia and I didn't know what to expect at the outdoor festival or where exactly it was set up. We drove there Friday night and found the location beforehand. The Festival would be held over the weekend and I would wrestle multiple times outdoors. We had a game plan of walking around the festival before the card started to get the word out for the matches and get some pictures with fans that I could also use for my Facebook page.

The following morning we arrived at the Festival early. The set up was crowded in a small tent crammed with wrestlers. I was determined to be professional and earn my money and the push I was being given by Todd. As Tia and I walked around in my gear with my new silver cape that her aunt Candy had made for me, Latin Thunder was a hit. We were constantly asked for pictures with children and adults alike. It was a good confirmation that my instincts were right about a lucha libre. The masked luchador was a great mix of showmanship, color, mystery, and Latino pride. My Spanish helped create an authenticity to the gimmick. People loved it. We were on the right track.

In the makeshift tent locker room as I got ready for my match with fellow Muscatine native Knight Wagner, I ran into Marek Brave. He was a sight for sore eyes. I hadn't seen Marek in years and didn't know he was back wrestling after he had suffered his terrible neck injury a few years back. He looked great, had cut his long hair, looked healthy, and was acting so mature that I almost rubbed my eyes to make sure it was really him! He told me he was married and had a toddler at home.

He was still a student of the game, as he watched every

match. He had grown as a wrestler like we all do as he was focused more on having a good match and not crazy spots. He went out and had a great match with an eighteen-year-old wrestler named Garret that was perfect. I couldn't help but see the irony of Marek being the heel and wrestling this white meat babyface. Ten years earlier Marek would have been the teenybopper baby getting sympathy from the crowd. He got great heat as the crowd got behind the underdog babyface. Marek and Krotch, a fellow Scott County Wrestling alumni who I had worked with in IPW, told me SCW was back holding cards. They had a good building in Walcott, Iowa, where they ran every month in front of a good crowd made up of a lot of families.

After my match with Wagner, I came back for a six man tag. Todd had me go over both times, and the crowd was into my new gimmick. After Tia and the kids left, I got changed and headed out. The tent was so crowded and the heat so intense that I really felt exhausted. It was the first time I'd ever truly felt my age. I couldn't relax in the tent, and I didn't want to walk around in the fresh air with my mask off. It was tough and I was relieved to get back to the hotel, shower, and then have a nice meal with everyone at the Iowa Machine Shed.

The next morning I contacted Todd and told him the heat and the tent made for a tough day. Was there something we could do differently? He was very accommodating and told me I could cut my matches down to one and make that a tag. I appreciated it, but told him the tent was the biggest challenge. So, we kept the singles match and I would wrestle the battle royal at the end. Todd told me to get there as late as possible and he would schedule my two matches as close together as he could, so I wouldn't have to be in the tent very long. I appreciated his understanding and Sunday was more enjoyable despite the relentless heat.

I was thrilled with how the Latino Festival went and the reception we got. I felt great when I was checking my Facebook and Tia shared a link on her page. We had made Fox News Latino! The national website did an article on the Latino Festival in Des Moines and the growing Hispanic population. The lead picture on the front was a shot of me standing on the ring ropes celebrating my victory. Out of all the pictures and images they took that weekend that was the photo an editor picked for the cover shot. Lucha libre really was a colorful symbol of the Latino community.

CHAPTER FORTY-EIGHT

My Hero Passes

I spent the rest of the fall working for IPW in Algona. My merchandise sales helped with the expenses of the trip as I used The Vault in Algona as a laboratory to perfect the gimmick. I debuted my new red and gold gear there.

I also learned more and more about being a Mexican masked luchador. Luis with Chilanga Mask helped me understand the mystique of the mask. He patiently explained how I needed to guard my identity. He said, "Keep your identity as hidden as possible. Don't walk around the arena with your mask off in your gear." Simple concepts that I needed to respect if I wanted to be a luchador.

I saw a great interview with El Hijo De Santo and Emilio Charles discussing the same concept. Emilio was bemoaning to Santo how the young wrestlers in Mexico don't respect the mask and its mystique. They would walk around with their mask off or take it off for young, good-looking girls. Charles implored the young wrestlers to follow the traditions the old timers did in Mexico. Charles had a son who had begun wrestling and, when Emilio accompanied him to a card, he told his son blocks away from the arena to put the mask on in the car. He was to walk into the arena with his mask on and never be outside the locker room with it off.

Emilio told the story of being on cards with Santo for over five years before he ever saw him with his mask off. He showered with a special mask on. Emilio said the first time he ever saw Santo with his mask off was their first international tour together where Santo had to go through customs unmasked. Santo said simply wearing the mask was a sacrifice.

I struggled with keeping my identity hidden in this day and age of social media. But, just like Delta when I tried to be a true heel, I found I could keep some of the fundamental concepts alive. I've begun to leave arenas with my mask on more and more. It can make you feel self-conscious and frankly a bit weird walking around in public with the mask but, as Santo said, its a sacrifice. It does add to the mystique. It works, just as the old timers said it did.

As 2013 wound down, I had a chance to reflect on my

journey in wrestling. I was having fun and taking my own advice to dream big. I set goals of wrestling internationally. I reconnected with the dreams of my youth where I hoped wrestling could show me the world. I had decided I would push to be booked in England and Ireland, as well as some states I always wanted to work in such as Oregon and Florida.

But shortly before Christmas, my world was rocked when I lost one of my biggest fans and my first and biggest hero in life. Dad passed away en route to Iowa City from a heart attack. He had suffered from heart disease for over a decade and each heart attack slowed him down more and more.

As my siblings and I spent time with mom preparing to honor him, I was so glad I had Tia and the kids in my life to lean on. My friends from work and wrestling were there to offer comforting words and help out any way they could.

Dad had given me a love for reading that had served me well over the years and had never questioned my wrestling dreams. He was an incredible father, always spending time with us and providing for his family. During the last conversation I had with him, he encouraged me to write my memoirs by saying, "You have something inside of you telling you to share this story, you need to write it."

I realized over the past couple years that dad had been very ambitious when he was younger. It took a lot of courage to leave the border and travel north. But he knew Eagle Pass had nothing to offer him, so he took his opportunity for a better life and paid the price at his hot, heavy, factory job. It had to have been hard being so far away from his beloved mother. But his ambition helped create a better life for all of his children and now grandchildren. It was the classic American immigrant experience. My siblings and I and our kids are enjoying the fruits of his labor and sacrifice. He had grown tired. Work, his age, and heart disease wore him down. But unlike so many blue collar men, we were thankful he enjoyed a decade of retirement and grandchildren.

CHAPTER FORTY-NINE

Meeting "Wildfire"

Myself with the legendary Mil Mascaras

When 2014 rolled in, I continued to refine the Latin Thunder character. I was determined to learn from my mistakes. I decided to think big, be patient, and keep my momentum going.

Tia and I went with some of our IPW family to the Cauliflower Alley Club's annual reunion. There I had the thrill of meeting Mil Mascaras for the first time! My friends ribbed me about how excited I was to meet him, but it was all in good fun. It was great to talk to Mil in Spanish and let him know how he inspired my character. Mil was kind enough to grant us an interview and had encouraging words for me.

I began writing my memoirs in March. I wrote my opening chapter right away on my very first memories of wrestling. Seeing Tommy "Wildfire" Rich and "Mad Dog" Buzz Sawyer tearing up the Superstation TBS studios in Atlanta began my lifelong love affair with the sport.

In late August while the book was being edited, I got a text from my friend Mike Ray asking me if I was interested in going with him to a wrestling show in the Quad Cities on Sunday night. Harley Race and Tommy "Wildfire" Rich were supposed to be there. I texted back that I was on graveyards, so I would be going in to work Sunday night at eleven p.m. I wouldn't be able to go to any event in the evening out of town. I was also skeptical. I hadn't heard anything about any wrestling show in Davenport. I also hadn't heard about my first childhood wrestling hero Tommy

Rich appearing at a show.

I was wrestling for SCW at the Bierstube Bar in Moline, Illinois, that same Saturday night. I was getting dressed when my opponent told me he was booked the following night for a show Harley Race was going to be at. I told him I'd heard about the card, but wasn't sure it was true. He said a local promoter Scott was bringing Race and Tommy Rich in.

"Cool," I said, "That's pretty awesome Tommy is going to be in the Quad Cities."

An hour later when I was getting warmed up for my match which was on third, the opening match guys made a comment about Tommy Rich. I asked, "Is Tommy Rich here?"

"Yeah, he's here with Scott," they replied.

Wow. Tommy "Wildfire" Rich was here. I'd met a lot of my wrestling heroes over the years, but never Rich. I didn't hide my excitement any more if I met one of my wrestling heroes. I was proud of being a fan and happy to tell veterans how many memories they made for me in my childhood.

Five minutes later Tommy Rich came walking up the stairs. I recognized that raspy Tennessee voice as soon as I heard it. I turned around and there was Tommy. His hair was still bleached blond and he retained some of his youthful features. I shook his hand and called him Mr. Rich.

Tommy told me, "Don't call me Mr. Rich. Every time I hear someone call me that I get the urge to throw my hands up in the air and freeze!"

I headed down the stairs to get on deck for my match, though all I wanted to do was sit and chat with Tommy. As "Wildfire" headed down the stairs towards me, his body struggled. His hips, knees, and back all looked to be in pain. Pain from the punishment he took all those years to entertain people like me. His fans.

He laughed as he struggled down the stairs and yelled half jokingly, "Catch me!"

I looked him in the eyes and with all seriousness told him, "I'll catch you, Tommy. Don't worry, brother. I'll catch you." I meant every word.

"Wildfire" Tommy Rich was the first man I saw on TV that grabbed me. His charisma and fire captured my imagination. Now I had a chance to tell him one-on-one at the bottom of those stairs as I shook his hand again how much he meant to my childhood. He was my Lone Ranger, my Mickey Mantle.

"How old are you?" Tommy asked.

"I was 9 years old when I saw you in 1982, Tommy. Channel 17, Gordon Solie, man I loved Georgia Championship Wrestling!"

"Well, you were just a little guy!" he answered.

We chatted a bit and then said goodbye.

Meeting "Wildfire" just kept me smiling all night. What a business.

All these years, the setbacks, the starts and stops, I wondered why I chased it. Why did I pick wrestling to pursue? I'm convinced now - it picked me.

Looking forward, I know the road ahead is much shorter than the road behind me. But hopefully I still have a few more years to enjoy this journey. The wrestling business has introduced me to wonderful characters and provided me so many lessons on life. I hope to spend the remaining years giving back and maybe providing a bit of inspiration to young people the way my bodybuilding and wrestling stars did for me as a teen.

I'm content to work for my wrestling family of IPW where my kids cheer their favorite wrestlers such as Nichole Lynn, Kiandra Benson, and James Jefferries. I also am thoroughly enjoying working for Marek Brave and the crew of Scott County Wrestling this year. I'm hoping to see a bit of the world in 2015 and a few years after before I hang up the boots.

I've loved being a part of it from the very beginning. Thank you for letting me share my journey with you.

If you enjoyed this book please consider writing a review on Amazon, Goodreads or your favorite platform. I hope you can visit www.latinthunder.com where you can continue reading about my journey on professional wrestling through my blog.

Battling Nate Alsin for IPW Photo: Miranda Cantrell

Lightning Source UK Ltd.
Milton Keynes UK
UKHW041820041218
333468UK00001B/304/P